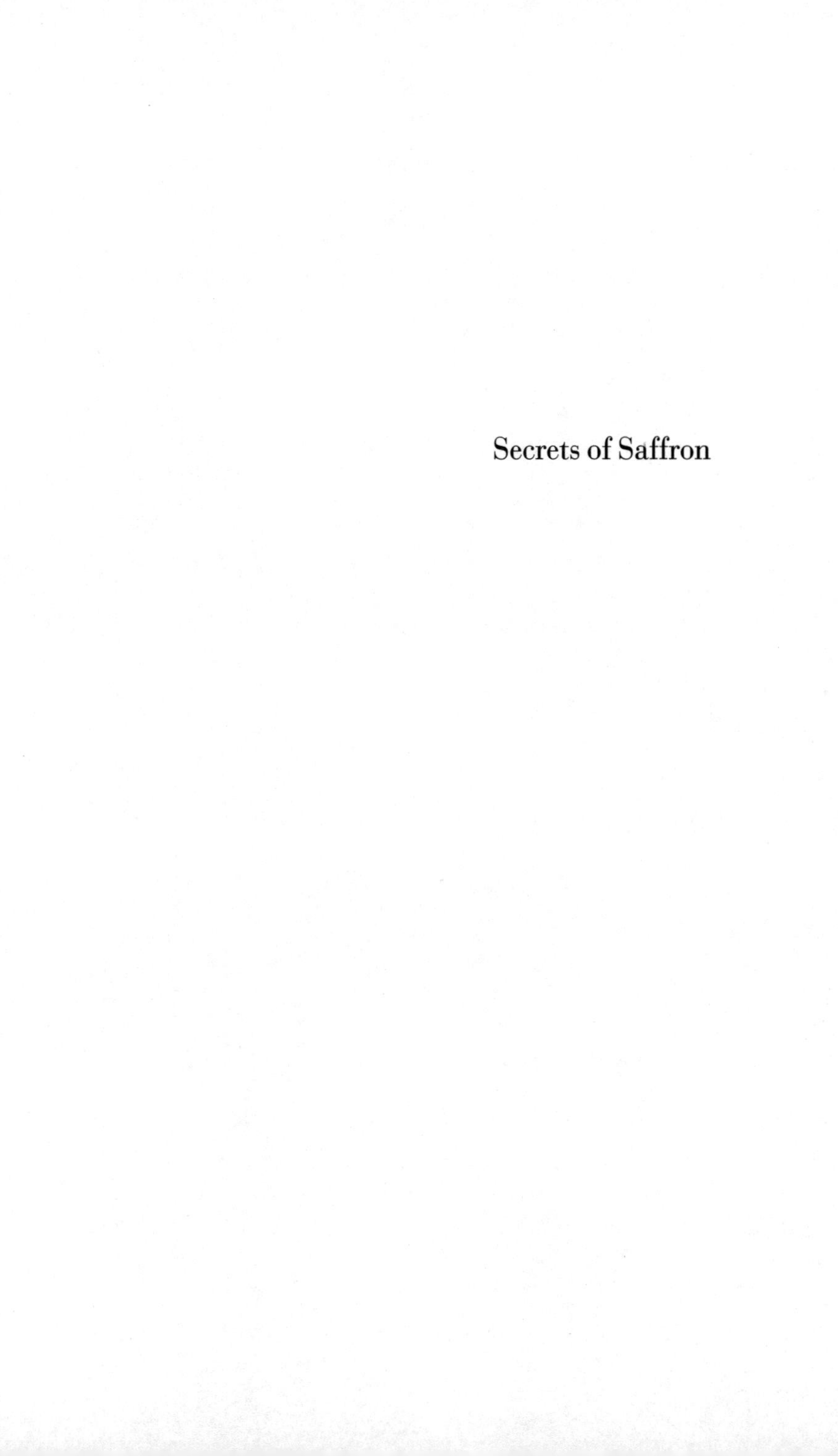

Secrets of Saffron

other books by Pat Willard

A Soothing Broth: Tonics, Custards, Soups, and Other Cure-Alls for Colds, Coughs, Upset Tummies, and Out-of-Sorts Days

Pie Every Day: Recipes and Slices of Life

PAT WILLARD

Secrets of saffron

THE VAGABOND LIFE OF THE WORLD'S MOST SEDUCTIVE SPICE

BEACON PRESS
BOSTON

Beacon Press
25 Beacon Street
Boston, Massachusetts
02108-2892
www.beacon.org

Beacon Press books
are published under the auspices of
the Unitarian Universalist Association of Congregations.

Printed in the United States of America
06 05 04 03 02 01 8 7 6 5 4 3 2 1

This book is printed on acid-free paper that meets the uncoated paper ANSI/NISO
specifications for permanence as revised in 1992.

Text design by Lucinda Hitchcock
Composition by Wilsted & Taylor Publishing Services

LIBRARY OF CONGRESS CATALOGING-IN-PUBLICATION DATA
Willard, Pat.
Secrets of saffron : the vagabond life of the world's most seductive spice / Pat Willard.
p. cm.
ISBN 0-8070-5008-3 (cloth)
1. Cookery (Saffron) 2. Saffron (Spice) I. Title.
TX819.S24 W55 2001
641.6'383—dc21 00-012039

for Chris

Contents

PREFACE

It will be obvious to anyone in just the first few pages that this is a highly personal take on the intriguing path saffron has taken through time. Although I thoroughly researched the background and details, much of what I am relating has been filtered through a screen of fiction. The most memorable history is essentially good storytelling, and while I have remained faithful and true to the facts, to secure the flavor of the characters and events, I have sometimes included dialogue and thoughts that are based solely on the whims of life and my experience of human nature. Scholars and historians may frown and quibble, but since I have never claimed to be more than what I present here, I hope in the long run they will just stretch back and enjoy the read.

Many may find it curious that a book about saffron leaves India almost entirely out of the telling. When people think of saffron, frequently they think of India along with Spain. Although both countries have a long tradition of cooking with the spice, it is not a native to either and was introduced by conquerors – the Moors in Spain and the ancient Persians in India. When I began to research saffron, I quickly came to realize that while each country had a complex history of using the spice, Spain's is a little more straightforward and connected to the book's themes, whereas India's is an intricate labyrinth, and to do it justice would require a book of its own. (Part of saffron's history in India would include its travels into China – a less well known journey, but an interesting one.) It would be rewarding to write that book as well.

A word about the measurements used in some of the recipes: I have maintained the terms given in the translations of many of the ancient texts. For instance, the Egyptian recipes found in the Papyrus Eber use the dirham, a unit of Moroccan currency, as a unit of measure. This is like saying "take 10 cents' worth of – ." Given that most of the recipes in which the dirham is used in this way also require obscure or impossible-to-find ingredients with no known modern equivalents, it is very hard to prepare the recipes. I have included them, though, for their beautiful and poetic language, as well as for their historical significance.

Please note that the medical recipes given in this book are given solely for historical purposes. I do not recommend that anyone try even the most innocent-sounding ones. I do not think any of these medicinal recipes would be harmful in and of themselves, but it is dubious whether they will cure the illness they were intended to, and relying upon them rather than consulting a doctor could do real harm.

One final note, and it is one of gratitude: Thanks to Mary Ray Worley for her fine copyediting of the final manuscript and to the two women who truly pulled me through the last hard months – my agent, Anne Depue, for her constant good judgment, cleverness, and insight, and my editor, Tisha Hooks, for her gentle yet steely support and faith when I, myself, had none. Thanks, girls.

Secrets of Saffron

INTRODUCTION

The Heart of the Matter

Crocus and Smilax may be turn'd to flow'rs,
And the Curetes spring from bounteous show'rs
I pass a hundred legends stale, as these,
And with sweet novelty your taste to please.
OVID, *Metamorphoses*

How the nymph Smilax – eternally radiant, never to wither under the cold blast of age – dealt so capriciously with the tenacious nature of a mortal lover:

A handsome youth named Crocus was passing through the Athenian forest on his way to his parents' house when he spied the nymph Smilax dancing in a clearing with her friends. As is the way with nymphs, they called a coy welcome to him, and he returned their greeting, though surely he must have hesitated a bit, hampered by an awkward reserve before such abundant beauty. And yet he could not help gazing at them and, in gazing, distinguishing Smilax as the fairest. It does not take much for a nymph to encourage a man; her youth, her suppleness, her gaiety only magnify the sense of rapture that surrounds her, and that was enough for Crocus to relinquish his heart. Did he and Smilax exchange many words? Did they speak of what was in their souls? Of course not; he had lived far too few days and she too many for anything but the moment to matter. And so Crocus began to haunt the forest, and for a time, Smilax, alone and unattended, allowed him to find her.

To be worshiped by a mortal gives a nymph as much a taste of power as she will ever possess. What did she care that he began to neglect his parents, his friends, the chores he had at home, just for the sake of being near her? He would not hear from anyone – not his father and heartbroken mother, nor his boyhood friends – how much trouble a nymph could bring. Each day he went into the forest, and each night he left more bewitched than before.

But soon, far too soon, Smilax grew weary of him; his adoration became a nuisance to her. It was once a sweet pleasure to let a handsome human run his hands down her body, but now she longed to be away with the other nymphs, to dance and feast and swim with them in the deep cool forest brooks. But Crocus was not easily thwarted – even by her. And so he continued to go into the forest to seek her out, until at last Smilax turned peevish and transformed him into a small purple flower with a fiery heart.

There are so few places in the world where saffron grows naturally that its origins in an ill-tempered girl and her bothersome sweetheart must have made a certain sense. Most spices come from the Far East, but this – the most precious spice of all – thrives only where a hot Mediterranean breeze rakes across arid ground. Primeval traces of saffron are found in the pigment of prehistoric beasts painted on the cold walls of Iraqi caves and in tattered threads pulled from disintegrating carpets and funeral shrouds of the ancient Persian court. Monkeys and young girls gather it on palace frescoes in Crete; legendary accounts survive of sailors risking their lives along the Balkan shores and down the rocky southern coast of Cilcia where the finest saffron was thought to be found.

In this small circle of the world – and in no other – does saffron flourish of its own accord. Wherever else the crocus bulb has grown, it arrived in the pockets of conquering armies or the leather pouches of thieves and traders, those who could not do without its potent taste or saw in its arduous rarity a chance for riches. To succeed, however, the crocus bulb must find in foreign soil a replica of its ancestral homelands, and so it has rarely settled far from the Mediterranean shore. The ideal spot for a saffron field stretches south, in a climate of strong summer heat and steady winter cold, with nothing to shield the ground from the sun. The soil must be rich, well dressed, carefully tended; the air dry, even a little parched. In the month of June, the plain little knuckle-sized brown corms are buried deep, as many as the ground will hold, and then – except occasionally to weed and, if necessary, to water the field – there is nothing left for the saffron grower to do.

The summer deepens and the world goes on about its business. While the neighboring fields are tilled and cultivated and harvested, the saffron corms mask themselves as pretty flowers. Spindly green leaves and the tips of tightly wrapped buds gradually appear, embedding the saffron plains with tiny purple spikes. Through the long hot summer days, the sun's heat and the earth's strength are slowly siphoned into the tight confines of the spike's core. It is not until everything else has gone to seed, after showier specimens have spent their beauty in summer's heat and there is scarcely a temperate breath remaining in the October sky, that the saffron crocus unfurls in a burst of sudden purple radiance, the dawning light revealing the splendor dancing amid the surrounding fallowed landscape.

A cry lets out, the bells ring, and workers rush into the fields, shuffling up and down and across the rows of blossoms, gathering as many as they can before the midday sun wilts the crocus's petals and melts its sated heart. And it is the heart – the three plump trumpet-shaped stigmas and a bit of white style – that has for thousands of years been the prize. Such fragile potency makes the harvest fast and brutal. The one or two weeks during which the flowers bloom – three blossoms for each corm, opening on succeeding mornings – require Herculean drive. Fingers gnarl and backs begin to ache. Eyes grow weary; skin stains a burnt orange hue. It is delicate work and has, so far, resisted modern machines and innovations. For that reason, saffron is most at home in rustic pockets of insular countries. With the mainstay crops already gathered for the winter, the tedious work is accomplished by needy farmers who consider saffron a small but dependable investment. The exhausting industry necessary to produce even the faintest amount of saffron is performed more often than not in the pleasant anticipation of the high price and eager buyers the spice commands. Yet, a little is always reserved from the harvest – a private store that the farmers hoard for themselves.

And that is the reward for the tired workers. Beyond its great economic worth, there is the anticipation of what saffron generously bestows to even the meanest of circumstances. In the dying embers of the autumn day, while the thin filaments of the crocus's heart are laid upon a screen to dry, the rising scent imparts venerable dreams of feasts to come; the ruddy hue staining weary fingertips a pale reminder of summer's sunsets to toast chilling bones.

I do not know who first stirred saffron into a cup of water to use as paint or dye, or rouge a pouting mouth or burnish a broth for the evening meal, but I do know a little about how saffron warms chilled bones. I felt my own begin to thaw the first time I truly tasted the spice. It was in a northern city by the sea, and from the high window of the house where I was staying, I could see ice floes in the harbor bobbing up and down among the steely waves. The three little rooms behind me were frigid. In the narrow front room neat rows of paperback books lined the wall, a good typewriter sat on a small wooden table by the window, and in a corner stood an old and curiously fancy wooden wheelchair. Its high back was intricately caned, framed in garlands of carved wooden leaves and roses; on the arm and foot rests it appeared as if drops of blood had been rubbed into the grain. In another room off to the side a wide mattress lay on the floor, and it, too, was surrounded by rows of books. Both of these rooms were dark, heavily curtained by the branches of overgrown fir trees that constantly brushed against the windows and over the gabled rooftop

The brightest room was the one you entered first – a large kitchen with a sink, an old stove, and an even older refrigerator. But there was a long wooden table down the center with comfortable chairs surrounding it, and three wide windows facing the barren expanse of the harbor and the sea.

I did not belong in these rooms. The books – all fine American classics – and the mattress, the one skillet, and the enormous stockpot, and especially the wheelchair, belonged to a couple I knew at the university. With the good will of a rich aunt, they were in Bermuda, and I was paying their January rent while I looked for a place of my own.

I also took the rooms so I could have a quiet place to work, as well as to be with the man I had fallen in love with. But a week after I moved in, he was given a co-op assignment in a city two hours away, and I was so cold and lonely and spooked by the wheelchair and the fir trees always sweeping the windows that instead of looking for an apartment or doing any work I fell sick. I spent the days coughing and wheezing in the kitchen, listening to the couple's albums and the radio when I needed to hear another human voice. I lived on oatmeal and tea and spent hours pondering my misery.

And that was how a friend of the couple's found me when he showed up one afternoon looking for them. I had met Michael during my first semester at the university. We took a writing class together, for which he wrote brilliantly funny stories and fought with the teacher whom he admired but did not like. He was tall and thin in an undernourished, intense way and was always rushing off with other people to readings and bars. I never had the courage to talk to him; I admired his work, but he often appeared surly. By the next semester he was gone, and he did not return the following fall.

But here he was now, looping uninvited into the kitchen and sitting down at the table while I remained at the open door with an old blanket wrapped around my long rosebud-printed flannel nightgown. He asked about his friends, and I explained that they were in Bermuda. He took that in, and after an awkward pause, when he did not get up from the table, I offered him some tea, which he accepted. I put the kettle on, got another mug down from the shelf, cut my last orange into equal quarters, and scrounged up a plate of crackers. It was a lustrous winter day, the sun splintering off the snow on the surrounding rooftops to refract across the kitchen floor in warming struts. Michael devoured every last orange slice while he told me quickly how he was just back from Alaska, where he had been working on a salmon boat and then at a fish-processing plant. He stretched out his hands to show me his tapered fingers scarred from hooks and nets and scaling knives. He looked older than I remembered. His hair was long, blond yet almost grizzly around his gaunt face. But he seemed stronger, his shoulders and arms muscular, as if he had been whittled down to where only his mettle showed. When the tea was made, I set the mug down before him and then took a chair across the table.

"Did I wake you?" he asked after a while.

I shook my head. "I've been sick."

"With what?"

"I don't know."

He reached his hand across the table and placed it gently over my forehead. I could feel the calluses on his palms and fingertips press against my skin.

"You have a fever," he said. I told him I was taking aspirin.

"There's something better," he replied and quickly finished his tea. "Get into bed and I'll make it for you."

I did not know this man and felt I should be alarmed by him. What did I know of him beyond the few stories of his I had heard? And now here he was, fresh from the wilderness, ordering me to bed. But there was something in his manner – a distance and a caution – that allayed my reserve. I wrapped the tattered blanket around my shoulders and did as I was told.

Michael stayed behind in the kitchen, and after I lay down on the mattress I heard something banging down on the stove. The refrigerator door opened and closed. Cans and boxes were shifted across the open shelves. Then his footsteps trailed toward the apartment door, and the lock clicked behind him as he left. I was already half asleep and did not have the energy to call after him. The old window beside the bed funneled the cold wind across the mattress, and I burrowed down deeper under the layers of feather quilts, woolen blankets, and knitted afghans.

I awoke to darkness, not knowing how long I had slept. The door to the room had been shut, and a pungent, spicy scent that cut through my stuffy nose infused the air. I struggled out from under the blankets, turned on a lamp, and peered into the long mirror propped up against the wall across from the mattress to see what a mess I was. The radio was playing softly on the other side of the door while I changed into jeans and an old sweater.

"Good," Michael greeted me when I walked into the kitchen. He was at the table with an empty bottle of beer and an open book before him. The table was set with two bowls, big spoons, and a plate of sliced crusty bread. On the stove, the big stockpot breathed out thick vapors. I went to see what was inside and saw claws and shells covered in a red-tinged broth.

"What did you make?"

"Sit down," he commanded – not roughly or even insistently, though his voice was firm.

I sat down without knowing what it was I was about to eat or even really caring. I wasn't that hungry, and I was beginning to wish I was alone again. But the persuasive aroma from the pot melted my resistance. Michael filled my bowl and his too, then brought two bottles of beer from the refrigerator and shoved the book he was reading to the far end of the table. He shifted his bowl and utensils opposite from me and as soon as he sat down, we began to eat.

The broth was simply the juices from the shellfish, mixed with a little beer and powered by a healthy pinch of saffron. The vigorous flavor of the spice pierced the shells to permeate and heighten the delicate sweet flesh with a sharp bracing smack. While we ate, Michael began to talk more freely. He told me about how he went to Alaska thinking it would be different and how the men on the boats considered him a fool. He spoke a little about the writing he was trying to do, wondering if it was better to return to school or go back on the road again. I listened to him with a deeper interest than I had to any man for a long time, yet a part of me could not give up breaking through the shells and sucking at every last trace of meat I could find. When all the lobster and clams were gone, we tore the bread into the broth and let it swell with the juices, then slurped them up as hungrily as the shellfish. We finished our beers, and he got up to get us more. My fingers were florid and sticky, a sharp sting lingered on my lips, but there was a banking warmth in my belly. My head was clear, my fever dispersed.

Michael placed the new beers on the table and knelt down beside me, his arms resting along my thighs to clasp his hands on the back rungs of my chair. There was the flavor of saffron on his lips, on his tongue, when he kissed me. I smelled it on his fingers and in the weave of his sweater when I pressed my face against his chest. I was in love with another man, yet so much heat had invaded that room. It is nothing more than this, I contended, as I let him go on a little bit further: It is the saffron and the beer, the lobster and the clams, on a snowy wintry night in a northern city with ice floes in the harbor just beyond the frosty windows behind us. And then, like Smilax, I abruptly turned away from him – the worst and only thing I could have done – and when he left I would not see him again for years, when we were both older and different and without a trace of saffron.

Heaven and Earth

Go up to the ancient ruin heaps and walk around;
look at the skulls of the lowly and the great.
Which belongs to someone who did evil and which
to someone who did good?

SUMERIAN PROVERB

In the ancient valley kingdom of Sumer, between the Tigris and Euphrates Rivers, where some believe the Garden of Eden flourished, those who knew what to do with the curious flowers that bloomed after summer was forgotten would have been sanctified as priests or perfumers in service to one of the many temples or the royal court. They could have been attached to Inanna, who, as the contrary goddess of love, fertility, and (as if these were not enough to contend with) war, liked her carved images to be freshly anointed every day with opulent unguents and rare balms. Or they might have served the queen of the mountains, Ninhursag, who in a tangled bit of progeny was both the daughter of and consort to An, the king of heaven. Their union resulted in most of the other gods in the Sumerian heavens, a troublesome and demanding brew, susceptible to flattery and praise but often short-tempered and indifferent to mankind.

When Ninhursag wasn't with An, she whiled away the hours with Enki, the water lord, keeper of the divine laws, master of wisdom – and semen. Enki seems to have been a handful for even a goddess to manage. Known for his generous hospitality, he indulged himself too much in drinking and feasting, and this brought him only trouble. A few lamentable dalliances with several goddesses ended up populating the underworld; one ill-timed, unfortunate bender with the mother goddess Nimah while she was supposed to be molding humans from clay resulted in her fashioning several flawed human beings and letting them loose upon the world.

By all accounts, Ninhursag appeared to have been philosophical about these sorts of lapses, but she lost all patience with him when Enki proved himself a glutton and, in the span of one day, ate all of her sacred plants. Furious with him, Ninhursag banished him from the garden into the arid desert, where Enki slowly began to die, the eight organs inside his body where the plants had settled weakening as he fell upon the fiery sand in withering agony. A compassionate fox, seeing how he suffered, ran to Ninhursag and persuaded her to change her mind. She took her sweetheart back into the garden and lay beside him in the cool shade of a palm tree, bringing forth from his body a healing deity for each of his afflicted parts. For this reason, when Sumerians became ill they turned to their temples, where the men and women who served the deities knew how to mix potions and rubs – thick perfumes and bracing tonics – that would give praise to the gods who ruled their lives and who, thus placated, would sooth a mere mortal's troubled body.

Once it was discovered, saffron was used in many medicinal ways, and yet the flower was never considered worthy enough to cultivate. The Sumerians were a business-minded people, bureaucratic and methodical, who traded anything they thought they could turn a fair profit on, not only in the more primitive northern domains of Babylon and Assyria, but in the far eastern plains across the Zagros Mountains and southern seacoast, whose strange inhabitants the Sumerians regarded as just emerging from the ooze. Sumer's trading, and by extension its great preeminence long before the first pharaohs of Egypt thought to raise their pyramids – from 3800 B.C. to around 2000 B.C. – was a direct result of their skill in domesticating grains and fruit trees by fashioning irrigation channels to lead the river waters into arid fields. In the long, detailed inventories they meticulously recorded on tiny clay tablets found stacked like handfuls of bills and shopping lists among the buried ruins of their great cities, the most important commodities for sale were the barley and wheat they cooked into gruels and bread and, most especially, their much-beloved beer. But there were also acres of dates transformed into delectable sweets and a sticky, potent wine and honey stolen from wild bees and sold in huge pots. Up and down the Tigris and Euphrates plowed the Sumerians' wooden boats, brimming with flax and wool, with precious cedar wood, gold, copper, lapis lazuli, and ivory.

Yet, in almost eighteen hundred years of business dealings, they never once parted with their profusion of saffron threads. The reason why may be discovered under the mountains of business tallies the Sumerians left behind, for here among the corporate ledgers were recipes for remedies and potions – the world's first extensive medical texts. These they shared with their less learned neighbors – such as the Lullubus, Amorites, and Semites – but the herbs and spices they used in the recipes remained wild in the fields because they were deemed useless without the divine intervention of the deities.

The Sumerian gods and goddess were a demanding, obstinate lot, and the things they made humans do for them were often outrageous. You could sacrifice a ram and burn its body on a bed of fragrant cedar, or lay a feast of fish and bread dripping with date syrup on a golden cloth studded with rare shells from the far northern sea. You could even bring your young daughter to the temple for the priests to use as consort during the New Year ritual that assured the coming year's harvest – in which the priests would take turns being the resurrected fertility god Dumuzi while she would stand in for the goddess Inanna and offer her virginity to each and every one. You could do all this and maybe, just maybe, one of the gods would heed your pitiable plea, but you could never be sure what exactly would get their attention or how long you would hold it. And so the medicines and potions the Sumerians devised were fashioned more for their god-pleasing scent and beauty than for any of their curative powers, their worth, at best, of tenuous measure.

Yet every illness was taken seriously and treated as a matter of concern for the entire kingdom. The spiritual and physical realms were believed to be tightly woven together, and a king's headache or a shepherd's indignant belly could very well signify the universe's crumbling demise. Such a fragile world required careful handling; nothing was left to chance and everything was called into account.

Word of illness, great and small, was quickly conveyed to the temple, and the priest, accompanied by the doctor and a seer, would immediately set out to make a house call. As they walked along, they examined everyone and everything they passed, looking for omens and discussing their meanings. When they arrived at the sick person's house, the doctor examined the patient, the priest began to chant, and the seer questioned the family about any unusual occurrences and poked among their possessions for more clues to the misfortune. After the doctor mixed up some medicine, the seer would predict whether the cure would work. Sometimes the cure actually seemed to work; probably just as often it didn't, but if the seer had predicted a cure and none had occurred, then the patient was removed to a special room in the temple – the world's first hospital – where the walls were painted with beneficial incantations and more forceful offerings were made to the restive deities for their prompt intervention.

Most Sumerian medicines read like perfume recipes. Sometimes the ingredients were pounded into a paste and spread over the body above the offending organ; other times they were diluted with beer and drunk. One of their most common medicines, taken to strengthen and warm the stomach, was recorded in *Early Arabic Pharmacology,* by Martin Levey (Brill, 1973):

> *Take 10 dirhams of burnt pomegranate seeds; 3 dirhams each of seed of myrtle, oak, and sumac, cumin which has been macerated in vinegar, then burnt, flour of lotus fruit, flour of sorb, burnt coriander, Nabaten carob, Syrian carob, and 2 and a half dirhams of burnt saffron and 5 dirhams of burnt aloes. All are pulverized roughly and mixed [with strong beer].*

Before the spices were added to the beer (and the Sumerians would have made sure it was one of their more potent brews), the pounded mixture was the color of a newly unfolded marigold and emitted the crisp, sharp pollen scent of a summer field. It was hoped that when the fire's heat released the aromatic nature of the seeds, bark, leaves, and flowers, the gods and goddesses would be lured to the sickroom and, thus beguiled, attend to the invalid's needs as well as Ninhursag did for Enki.

Almost all of the recipes required the ingredients to be cooked, smashed, and pulverized – if not burned. Some were marinated for months on end, and others were kneaded with honey and sesame seeds into a thick odorous paste. One of the most beautiful recipes – both for its language and for its fragrance – was written by Tapputi-Belatekallim, a royal perfumer for the legendary king Gilgamesh, who took the throne around 2600 B.C. It is a salve she made for her king's aching legs, and it begins with her walking out at dawn across the dewy plains by the temple at Eridu to gather her ingredients.

> *At first light, I gather balsam from the forest, saffron hidden in the dusty grass, flowers from the river's left bank, essential oils of the fir cone, oil from the calamus root, and a young turtle's shell ground up fine. Blessed with balsam's heat, on the altar do the flowers burn, until the heavens hear our plea, then they are crushed and stirred: For seven sunrises and seven sunsets does the mixture purify, and then it is rubbed upon the limbs and while singing praise, as this is proper toward the god.*

A king, as much as his subjects, was still at the mercy of the gods' whims, and if he died, then saffron might well have been used for yet another purpose. Of all the ingredients listed in the Sumerian medical texts, only saffron comes with a dire warning that would echo down through the ages: the smell and taste were both addictive, and if it were ingested or inhaled too much, death would surely follow.

When the king or queen died, members of the royal court dressed in their finest linen robes and wove in their hair the most elaborate golden ribbons. With a small golden cup carried in their hands, the court followed their ruler down into the burial chamber. Soldiers lined the sloping passageway; court musicians played on their jewel-encrusted harps; servants led ox-drawn wagons and chariots laden with food, drink, and weapons. The royal corpse, robed and coiffed as it had been in life, was placed on its side in a magnificently domed vault. At some signal, the royal court, along with the soldiers, musicians, and servants, raised their golden cups to their lips. Mixed with the beer or wine was something that worked swift and sure, for the bodies fell quickly, hands still grasping cups and spears, fingers fanned out across harp strings, faces unmarked by struggle or even horror, not a gold ribbon disturbed by an agonizing shudder. When all was still, someone came to slit the oxen's throats, and then the burial chamber, with all its inhabitants, was sealed for eternity under dirt and stone.

After more than a thousand years of being washed in salty river water, the Garden turned to dust. Babylon and Assyria found their young legs and overcame their weary neighbors in unmerciful battles. The great palaces were ransacked; the immense ziggurats smashed; the defeated Sumerians assimilated or sent into slavery. These new warrior kingdoms were far too busy in their fierce and often cruel expansions to regard saffron any differently from what they had been taught when they were ruled by Sumer's kings. Originality and inventiveness do not often flourish in a hurly-burly mind but favor instead a more inward gaze and leisured bent. And so it was left to the Persians, those strange people along the southern sea and across the eastern plains, to discover the flower's true worth.

During the time when the Sumerians ruled the world, different tribes and clans from the far northern and eastern steppes wandered onto the unpromising plateau that spreads below the Zagros Mountains. No one knows why they came, but the ones who stayed were drawn together by an extraordinary capacity to look upon the flat, blistering stretch of ground and recognize the raw outlines of an earthly paradise. Certainly they were guided by a religion that was born in fire, where the soul was composed of radiant light and the promised Messiah would one day walk upon the land. Through happy accident, by the beginning of the second millennium B.C., all these divergent people settled together at once. For a very long time, they had no one ruler to consolidate them under one sword and stop the invading troops from rampaging through their early settlements. No one man or clan rose up to distract their vision with empire building. And so, gradually, they drew together, becoming singularly attune to the slim graces of this bleached and stony terrain. With intelligence and imagination, they mastered each other's native skills and gradually filled their adopted homeland with color and scent.

At first, these people simply sought a measure of comfort in the desert kingdom they came to call Parsa. Rugs had been made for centuries before the Persians began to weave their own, but in their hands rugs turned into dazzling fields. The rugs were first made of felt – matted hair from native sheep whose tails were so long and fat that they dragged on the ground behind them like giant clubs. But felt wears quickly and falls apart, and so the Persians began to spin wool into thick threads that they then wove and knotted together. In the tattered remnants that have survived their burial in dark tombs, it has been found that even these early rugs were as lush as long grass and as beautiful as a meadow, warm in the months when the wind screamed down the mountainside and protective during the days the ground was transformed into a searing bed.

From the beginning, though, Persian rugs were very colorful. Western tribes from India taught the Persians how to draw color from all kinds of insects, fish, plants, and even rocks. In this landscape between pale lavender mountains and salt white deserts, the deeper, more vibrant shades of blue, purple, red, and yellow were desired most. To make blue, they shredded leaves from the indigo plant; for violet, young boys and men ventured to the sea and cut from the rocks the stubborn murex shells. For reds, there were many choices: kermes (the dried bodies of various insects) or, if kermes were out of season, then madden roots could be used. And if the madden roots had all been gathered, lichen was scraped from trees and fermented into a smelly, bloody paste. For yellow, there were several possibilities as well: various berries, pomegranate rinds, and wild plums. But if the most lively yellow was desired, one that yielded all the brilliance of the noonday sun, then only the saffron crocus would do. So much was it coveted – so important was this shade to the rug makers – that, for the first time, whole tracts of barely workable land were cleared of scrub, the hard, dry soil cracked open, and millions of saffron corms harvested from the wild were carefully transplanted in neat and narrow rows.

Once the vapors from the rug makers' hot dye baths were inhaled, it was only a matter of time before the Persians found other uses for the tiny crocus threads. In a hot, sweaty country, what was most attractive about saffron after its property as a dye was its scent. Its clean sharpness, clinging lightly to everything it touches, as alluring and elegant as a thin veil, would have been hard to resist. Soon, saffron was being scattered across the bed at night, freshening sheets and pillows, inducing a tranquil sleep. Persians swore that a cup of saffron tea relieved their melancholy; a pouch of it worn on a string around the neck and dangling above the heart would enkindle love. During the burning months when hot breezes brushed across the shadeless plateau, saffron and sandalwood were stirred into water that was left in a bowl beside the front stoop to wash the dust and heat from parched bodies.

And often saffron was planted in secluded gardens, not only for a private ready crop but also for the unassuming, guileless charm of its petite flowers. In this long period of quiet advancement, while the kingdom bided its time, learning as it watched the ever-rumbling turmoil that wreaked havoc in neighboring countries, Persians concentrated on making their lives more comfortable and meaningful – pursuing pleasures that, in fifteen hundred years would influence, even conquer, the rest of the world. Not least of these pleasures were the gardens they created. The Persians called them *pairidaezas* – small paradises, framed by the walls of individual houses and laid out in orderly geometric patterns to bring balance and succor into a harsh world. One of nature's paradoxes is that the most lush and perfumed flowers are often happiest in the driest, sunniest, soil, and in the small oases and thin strips of fertile land that dotted the countryside, roses, lilies, and jasmine grew naturally in enormous profusion. Behind their garden walls, the Persians transplanted these flowers within a precisely plumed box sketched with lemon and pomegranate trees, the flowers in their tidy rows separated by tall, thin spikes of cypress, framed by the graceful arch of musky wild grasses and bordered by irises in the summer and saffron in the fall.

Surrounded by saffron, then, how long could it have been before an ingenious cook tossed it into a bowl? It would have been, of course, a royal cook, someone who prepared food not only to survive but also to enjoy, someone who would consider the possibility of infusing scent and color into a pallid cuisine a magnificent accomplishment. The Persian royal family, with time enough to meditate on such matters, expected their food to be more than just flavorful. Why, they asked, couldn't their meals be as fragrant and beautiful as everything else in life? For if they could – if, for instance, a routine plate of warm eggs or rice could suddenly beguile the nose and eyes – would not hunger then permeate all the senses, and in such a heightened state, would not satisfying such a hunger be a most rare experience, beyond the reaches of what a warm egg or bowl of rice had ever satisfied before? And if this was so, would not eating be transformed into something more – into a perfect communion of almost religious intensity?

Soon enough, aristocrats in the court followed suit, and it was not long before lower cooks and insignificant servants were gathering their own saffron to stir into their family's meals. In the twilight cool of the day's end, on a soft rug spread under a tree in the garden, royal and common families alike would settle around small bowls filled with delicacies – almond-sweetened lamb, chicken tart with pomegranate juice, figs so ripe that their tender, softened flesh seemed about to burst through its leathery skins. Thick goat milk was sharpened with mint, and the rice gleamed like amber, each grain plump with a melodious sweetness. Far away from the aggressive strife that prevailed in surrounding kingdoms, the Persians ate with slow, deliberate relish, pausing to breath the jasmine-scented air, to listen to the birds settle for the night in the upper branches of the almond trees, to appreciate in the murmur of their private paradises this exquisite union they had wrought between earth and heaven.

The Artist's Palette

Spend the day merrily, O priest.
Put unguent and saffron oil together to thy nostrils,
and garlands and lotus flowers to your beloved's
body.

ANCIENT EGYPTIAN BANQUET SONG

I.

I want to live in the palace of Knossos on the island of Crete. I want to be tightly corseted in a Minoan's saffron-yellow bolero jacket made from the lightest wool, the embroidered edges of the open bodice stiffened to raise my exposed breasts toward the sun's hot glaze and the sea's cool breath. I will paint my nipples with gold, anoint my long black curls with lily-scented oil. The gaily printed flounces on my long skirt will bell around my legs as I stroll through the labyrinth halls painted with leaping dolphins, gamboling blue monkeys, and gift-bearing men of impossible blithe beauty.

Here is where I would be, afloat in the Mediterranean, safe from all the marauding civilizations that plagued the surrounding mainland. Fifteen hundred years before the birth of Christ, there was no more peaceful kingdom on earth than Crete, protected as it was by legions of renowned sea monsters that kept acquisitive armies from venturing to navigate too far away from their own familiar shores.

Within this splendid isolation, Crete formed a culture of exquisite charm. The fortunate people who happened upon the island thousands of years before (from about 4000 to 3000 B.C.) had long ago blended together under a single language and similar customs, worshiping a matriarchal god who gave birth to a fertile world and whose young son, Zeus, died each year to be reborn in the ample harvest of the land and sea. The island, in those early days, was lush with cypress and cedar trees. There were spacious pastures, thick olive groves, acres of vineyards, and fields of wheat and barley. While their fleet of superb boats patrolled the surrounding waters against pirates and made sociable calls to their good friends – and rumored cousins – in Egypt, the citizens of Crete had no need of the outside world. Everything they wanted, everything they desired, was near at hand.

Surely, humanity's nature being what it is, there must have been some strife, but you would be hard pressed to find a trace of it in what was left behind. If you walk the length and breath of the island, you will not find the wreckage of a single fortress nor see a mountain peak defiled with tributes commemorating great battles and captive clans. You won't stumble upon the rubble of kingly edicts carved in stone or a ruler's toppled colossus proclaiming for all eternity regal might. This archaic land isn't even spoiled by shattered temples. The landscape where the people worshiped their goddesses and gods is as silent as the bones that lie beneath the vaulted nub of austere burial mounds.

Not even the clay tablets the Minoans left behind reveal their stories, since their writing has proved hard to translate. What has often been relied on instead are the legends and tales the Greeks recorded hundreds of years after Mycenaean warriors besieged the island and crushed its people.

Where the Minoans' spirit remains is in the ruins of their private homes – both humble and grand – on whose walls are rendered a world in which the human inhabitants and nature coexisted in sublime harmony. Captured by artists of rare sensitivity and astonishing talent, athletic men and elegant women of sloe-eyed charm are portrayed in sublime revelry. They dance and play, commune with deities in private ceremonies, celebrate the vitality and strength of bulls, and everywhere show their delight in their country's radiance – in its fields of wavering lilies and knots of precious saffron, with swallows flittering across sapphire skies and dolphins frothing the all-encompassing seas.

Undoubtedly, such amenable inclinations were further encouraged by the Aegean climate. The winter months are short in Crete, but they are often charged with freezing gales and salty snowstorms; the summers are longer but infused with an unbridled heat that clings like thick syrup to everything it touches, making bodies palpable, receptive to a more leisurely, even limpid order. After the brutal winter chills, the industrious Minoans must have hailed the summer with jubilant abandonment, for these months were full of activity and raucous celebration. On ordinary days, the farmers in their fields gathering wheat and picking olives, the shepherds tending their sheep, and the artisans at their pottery wheels, seated at their looms, bent over their jewelry benches, and mixing their pots of paint and lime clothed themselves in little more than sparsely draped loincloths and thin skirts. But for the many festivals that occurred at this time of year, the men wrapped short white kilts tightly around their pinched waists, then fastened on intricately designed codpieces – some made with gaily painted stiffened linen, others fashioned from silver covered in tin and hammered with sacred images. Some wore turbans on their heads; princes and noblemen owned fanciful headdresses of feathers, gold, and beads and oiled their dark hair to a high sheen, letting it stream in wavy curls down their sinewy backs.

The women wrapped their hair in colorful strings of beads and pearls, leaving long, thick ringlets to frame their face. They slipped on fine, almost transparent wool skirts tiered in colorful, pleated flounces of yellow, blue, white, and red, then laced themselves into snug yellow-tinted jackets that supported and left bare their full breasts. Cheeks and pouting lips were often rouged; for high court and religious ceremonies, nipples were painted gold. If they would be sitting in the sun – for a performance in the outdoor theater, perhaps, or on a balcony overlooking the palace road where athletes raced – they put on pretty picture hats, wide-brimmed bonnets to protect their fair white skin.

On palace and household walls, these posh fashions with their saucy displays of breasts and cocks appear more consecrated than erotic; in the Minoans' veneration of the natural world, the beauty of the human body, along with the miracle of its fertility, were intertwined with the sacred, even mysterious benevolence of the earth. Minoan women held a particular high status, revered above men for their life-giving abilities, yet equals and active participants in everything else.

For nearly sixteen hundred years – from about 3000 B.C. to 1450 B.C. – the Minoans flourished in this uniquely artistic, benevolent, and elegant society before a series of swift and terrible events bore them away into a long oblivion. Yet, as you wander through the labyrinthine halls of Knossos, following the path that Theseus navigated with his spool of thread, the shafts of light that pierce through the narrow windows and low doorways of the central court continue to illuminate the ravishing, animated faces of men and women exalting in a munificent life.

II.

Knossos, as well as the smaller palaces across the island, functioned as temple, town hall, storehouse, sports arena, and royal residence, and while certainly large and majestic, it was no more functional or ingeniously designed than many of the island's more plebeian homes. Crete houses were constructed around an inner courtyard, with thick, windowless exterior walls that denied entrance to winter's harsh cold and summer's brutal sun. Windows on the interior walls facing the courtyard let light and air into the spacious quarters inside. Shrines to the gods were placed everywhere, but the main sanctuary would be on the first floor, perhaps to make it easier to give offerings in the course of the day's comings and goings. Large storage rooms were also on the first floor, filled with giant earthen jars of olive oil and wine, along with bundles of wool to spin and wheat to thresh. The domestic areas were upstairs, attached to open porches and shaded roof tops where breezes from the sea could best be enjoyed. There were even bathrooms, furnished with large, commodious tubs, and toilets equipped with very modern-looking (and, in some ruins, still working) plumbing.

Even in the humblest homes, the interior walls were coated in lime plaster and, while still wet, painted with prismatic designs. In lesser rooms there was often only a simple border of interlocking red, purple, and yellow circles or delicately rendered ivy tendrils, or even blue surging waves. But, in the main apartments, every wall – from floor to ceiling – became the artist's canvas. The queen's chamber at Knossos was adorned with a frieze of darting dolphins amid schools of scattering fish; the four walls of a commoner's bedroom were found to be embellished with mountains blooming with tall, swaying lilies over which a flock of blue jays drifted. Life-size monkeys scampering through an orchard beside a winding stream filled a villa's large public room; in a stack of frescoes discovered lying on the floor – and appearing as fresh as when the house's owner painted them – another monkey was revealed. A fanciful reconstruction under the direction of Sir Arthur Evans, who began to excavate the ruins of Knossos in 1900, made the monkey out to be a handsome young boy, his supple waist and ankles encircled with gold harnesses, his nimble paws stealing saffron blooms from the palace's garden pots.

All of the frescoes are painted in such spirited, rich hues – the midnight blues and purples distilled from the mucous gland adjacent to the respiratory cavity of the *Murex brandaris* shellfish, the blood reds, auroral yellows, verdant greens scraped from oxidized metals – barely dimmed by either the island's strong sunlight or the passage of time.

Think, then, what it must have been like when these frescoes were freshly painted, to have lived among such exuberance! For peaceful coexistence, a person could not appear remotely retiring, and if homes were decorated so extravagantly, imagine how the Minoans must have arrayed themselves. It was not as if cosmetics and textile dyes were unknown in the world (there is evidence that the Minoans traded recipes and methods with their friends in Egypt soon after Neolithic times – long before either were ruled by kings), but on Crete the manufacturing, use, and applications of cosmetics and dyes were refined into a subtle art. Between these tightly related nations, what started out as probably a religious practice to ward off evil and make the body stronger developed into enhancements, and, at times, fabrication of natural beauty.

For cosmetics and textiles, the Minoans desired gentler and less permanent dyes than those used for frescoes. Harsh minerals and animal products were replaced by vegetables and flowers – and here is where saffron was employed. Crocuses grow most abundantly near the island's foothills, and although Crete did not cultivate the flower in neat rows the way Persia did, the Minoans must have carefully husbanded their natural supply to have gathered the flower in such great bundles. The fashion among Minoan women was to turn their skin as white as possible with maybe a dusting of chalk, to dot their high cheeks with bright rouge and paint their lips a deep red with pots of red ochre and saffron mixed with tallow, beeswax, or a little gum resin, then outline their large almond-shaped eyes with a thin stroke of kohl.

Where the Minoans in their fragmentary snapshots appear like restrained debutantes, the Egyptians in theirs are gaily – even at times outrageously – flamboyant. The Egyptians commonly heightened their natural bronze tone with henna diluted with a little saffron water and rimmed their eyes with a thick heavy coating of kohl – both to enhance their beauty and to ward off the sun's corrosive glare. On more festive occasions, men as well as women were given to mixing kohl with other pigments to produce shiny new colors – the deep blue, purple, and yellow shades that dazzle the eyelids in the portraits of the royal courts that line their tombs.

However, what both the Minoans and the Egyptians used with equal abandon was perfume. The sun bears down hard on Crete and Egypt, and given that there seemed to have been many convivial occasions for people to gather together, the perfumer's art would have been greatly appreciated. But these were also sensuous people, and the array of perfume recipes unearthed in the palace library of Knossos reveal the subtle art of using all the senses to attract. A master recipe for the queen's perfume reads as follows:

> *Saffron pounded in a crucible with myrrh until soft; mix with oil. Strain three times.*

The myrrh might have given the saffron a grassy edge – a little more complicated than the most popular perfume on Crete, which was made simply of rose petals steeped in water, then strained through a mild oil. When saffron threads were placed in the vials, the rose-tinged liquid turned a more pleasing shade of red. One perfumer was even adamant that saffron should always be added to the recipe since it deepened the fragrance of the rose petals and held it longer on the skin, "through the heavy motion of the sun's long day." On their own, though, the threads were often ground and packed in a pretty clay bowl to be dusted across the legs and feet with a couple of feathers tied together – a silky, aromatic talc to dry and cool the skin.

Almost all Egyptians were sensitive to personal cleanliness and bathed three or more times a day. They liked their saffron perfume to be a little heavier, mixed with a thick oil – possibly tallow or the oil from the next-to-last olive pressing. Even though the Egyptians imported saffron from Crete (as well as from Syria and Babylon when they weren't at war with them), it could not have been that expensive or even rare, since small vials still sealed and with the perfume inside were found in abundance in the ruins of a village set up for the workers building Merneptah's tomb. More saffron was sprinkled on sweaty clothes and bed linens, freshening them with its clean, sharp scent. It was also mixed in the solid cones of fat both men and women wore on top of their heavy wigs to dissolve in fragrant drips through the fiery day.

Most of all, Egyptians valued saffron as a dye, probably first admiring its deep yellow glow on the Minoan women's boleros and the tribute-bearing nobles' codpieces. The longer a piece of cloth was kept in the saffron dye bath, the more intense the yellow shade would become. But even the deepest shade would inevitably fade, seeping away in the wash, evaporating in the strong sunlight. The Minoans didn't mind this much: while all their many flocks of sheep were essentially kept for wool, it was a lot of work and took a long time to spin and weave the thread into cloth, which made even the queen lucky to have more than a few garments in her wardrobe. When something new was desired, it fell more often to the dyer than to the weaver to produce a fresh creation, making novel with colored dips what had turned unfashionable and dull.

The Egyptians, on the other hand, wound their dead in bright saffron bindings and desired that the color last a little while longer. When the Minoans sailed into the Nile delta, they must have shaken their heads in puzzlement over the enormous edifices of the sphinx and the pyramids, the multitude of palatial temples, and the countless statues of pharaohs, their long shadows cooling the hot sand that lapped at their stone feet. Maybe the Minoans' wonder was tempered by a shot of envy, a dash of professional jealousy at such a display of artistic skill, but their feelings would have been more than a little touched with disdain, if not for the parade of grandiosity, then for the preposterous notion of immortal life. The Minoans viewed their own death as no more consequential – or insignificant – than the seasonal flourishing and demise of plants and lesser animals. Their deities did not require that temples be built for them, for they had instead the natural grandeur of caves, mountains, and streams.

Most important, though, was the Minoans' faith in the mortality of their young Zeus. This central tenet of their religion won them only scorn from subsequent races. Even Saint Paul, who should have known better, called them liars for believing that the son of a goddess would die and be reborn for the sake of all mankind. The Minoans laid their dead together in simple buildings, some robed in magnificent jewelry, accompanied by their favorite possessions. Most, though, seemed to have gone into the next world with little more than their burial gowns. Offerings were made, incense was burned before the tomb, but everything the Minoans saw in the world strengthened their conviction that human beings were only a small part of the universe. It must have been a strong factor in the way they conducted their lives – rejoicing in the supreme beauty and masterfulness of nature, knowing they played only a small yet integral part in the continuity of the world.

It is a measure of Egypt's and Crete's respect for one another that both nations overlooked the other's strange customs and that, as close confidants surrounded by hostile and in some respects more primitive countries, a profound ripple of appreciation continued to flow unimpeded between the two. On pyramid walls and papyrus scrolls, Egyptians speak of the Minoans with rare affection, and in Knossos library are many lists of the gifts they bestowed on Egypt, not as tributes but as acknowledgment of felicitous esteem.

Nonetheless, it is in the Minoans' and the Egyptians' use of saffron that their distinct temperaments are so clearly marked – as the Minoans employed it for its fleeting, refined charm, whereas the Egyptians suffused it with a more permanent and valued meaning. In the dyer's art, this meant that the Egyptians searched for a way to make saffron's yellow stay fresh for all eternity, eventually developing a method that required the use of urine. Who or what supplied the urine is not recorded, but its effect on the poor dyer is recounted in the Papyrus Anastasc: "The hands of the dyer reek like rotting fish, and his eyes are overcome by weariness."

To be sure, being a dyer was a hard profession, doubly so because one could not easily walk away from it. Not only did the dyer's hands smell, but also his skin – his arms and legs and, as he often worked half naked because of the heat, his chest as well – would be permanently stained a multicolor hue. Still, the compensations must have been good enough (and certainly there was always work) to keep people performing such a putrid trade.

When an Egyptian died, a member of the family brought linen to the dyer's yard, while the body was carried away by the embalmer to the *ibu* (the tent of purification) to be washed, then to the *wabet* (the place of embalming), where for at least a month the body lay curing on a bed of salt. If the family was wealthy, the cloth was specially woven into bandages of the finest quality and of great length. Sometimes, in a sort of ancient charity thrift shop arrangement, the linen was bought at a local temple from a supply that had been used to wrap the cult figures of the gods in their shrines – gently worn but surely blessed. Most families, however, brought the dyer their old bed linens – frayed and expendable. The linens were torn into strips between 2½ to 8 inches in width, then joined together to make one long strip of at least 16 yards. For a really well wrapped mummy, more linen was held in reserve – some to be ripped into tiny bits and used to puff out sunken cheeks and chest, while others were left whole for a final blanketing. Then the cloth was submerged in a yellow bath until it was a shade just the other side of a ripe tangerine. When it was dried, the family brought it over to the embalmer's house.

First the head was tied, one band around the jaw to hold it firm, and then another to fix the head straight above the shoulders. Toes and fingers (and for a man, his penis) each got separate wrappings; arms and legs came next, followed by the torso. Amulets and pieces of jewelry were pinned onto each layer of binding; magical spells, prayers, and incantations were written on the cloths. Resin from pine trees and gum resin from myrrh were poured over the bindings and soaked through the binding layers to the body, through the skin, to the empty cavity inside, where it dried into a glasslike substance, making skin, meat, and bones hard, black, and lustrous. When all the appendages were finally fixed in place, the final wrapping began. Men's arms often extended over their bodies, their hands protectively covering their dressed genitals; women's arms could be straight along their sides or crossed, just as protectively as men's, over their breasts. Each layer was held in place with strips running like figure eights around shoulders and hips. The final layer was one big piece of linen, a neatly tied shroud dyed in saffron until the reign of Ramses III and the beginning of the New Kingdom, when it began to be dyed a bright red and held secure by red leather straps. By the time of the conquest of the Nubian dynasty in 712 B.C., the final shroud was fashioned from a netting of tubular blue faience beads.

The last step in preparing the mummy for its arduous journey remained the same: up to four gallons of perfume and balms made of saffron, rose, myrrh, oakmoss, and balsam resin were poured over the entire body. Lungs, stomach, intestines, spleen, liver, and later the brain – but not the heart, the seat of all wisdom, which remained snug inside the rib cage – were similarly treated. (The Egyptians – getting it more precise, I think, than did subsequent philosophies – claimed that the brain was the site for all emotions, the percolating wellspring for all men's passions.) Ancient Greek historians – Herodotus and, four hundred years later, Diodorus Siculus – disagree about their preservation methods. Whereas Herodotus said that the entrails were pickled in salt along with the body, Didodorus claimed that the solution was simply spiced palm wine. Modern scholars not only side with Didodorus but also claim that if you run out of your usual supplies spiced palm wine makes a very good disinfectant.

Whatever else happened to the viscera, before they were purified and bound they were often examined by Egyptian doctors, who took great advantage of this most sacred of religious rituals to study human anatomy. Embalmers themselves, with their thorough knowledge of the body, often practiced medicine, performing surgery and mixing drugs for their living clients.

Not since Sumer were so many medicines prepared as they were in ancient Egypt. Other nations certainly had their cures, but they did not take the time to document them as extensively, nor with such precision, as the Egyptians did. Greek writers claim that the Minoans gave the Egyptians many medical prescriptions, including how to make a drug called *daukos,* which was reputed to cure obesity without any tiresome dieting restrains. Yet, the carefree Minoans would not have delved as deeply into the mysteries of the human body as did the Egyptians, who kept a keen eye on immortality.

On the whole, Egyptians took a more active role in their destinies, starting with a healthy living regime. Besides the several baths everyone took during the day, men and women alike shaved all the hair from their heads and bodies to minimize the dangers of bacteria and germs. Then came certain dietary restrictions, such as not eating raw fish, and strict guidelines for analyzing dreams to discover any misfortunes on the horizon.

To alleviate aches and pains, certain preparations were made. The Papyrus Edwin Smith relates what to do in case of wounds – those received in battle as well as in the course of everyday life. The Papyrus Eber is much longer and broader and includes everything from hair-replacement compounds (the Egyptians' practice of shaving their heads notwithstanding) and wrinkle creams to what is billed as "a delightful remedy against death" (half an onion mixed in froth of beer).This is the source of the famous prescription to treat a black eye with a slab of raw beef and the very sensible direction to eat figs and wash them down with beer for constipation. (The translation I stumbled upon is a particularly delightful one because the translator, one Cyril P. Bryan, felt compelled to put in so many funny asides and comments that reading it is a little like sitting in on a lecture given by a very witty but learned professor. The edition was printed in 1931 and is long out of print, but you may find it tucked into a nearby public library.)

Intestinal and digestive ailments, in fact, make up the majority of troubles addressed in the Eber papyrus. Like their Sumarian counterparts, Egyptian physicians considered saffron to be a very potent treatment for everything that had to do with the stomach. One of the finest Eber prescriptions – both for pinpointing exactly what is ailing the poor patient and for providing a potion that might still work today reads thus:

> *When thou examinest the obstruction in his abdomen and thou findest that he is not in the condition to leap the Nile, his stomach is swollen and his chest asthmatic, then say thou to him: "It is the Blood that has got itself fixed and does not circulate." Do thou cause an emptying by means of a medicinal remedy. Make for him:*
>
> wormwood ⅛ part
> elderberry 1⁄16 part
> sebesten ⅛ part
> sasa-chips ⅛ part
>
> *Cook in beer that has been brewed from many ingredients, strain into one thoroughly, and let the patient drink.*

If stomach pain had progressed to the point that internal bleeding was suspected, another remedy was recommended:

> *This drives out blood through the mouth or rectum which resembles hog's blood when it is cooked. Either make him a poultice to cool him in front or thou dost not prepare him this remedy, but makest for him the following really excellent ointment composed of:*

ox fat, saffron seed, coriander, myrrh and aager-tree

Crush and apply as a poultice.

Saffron was also recommended to regulate the urinary tract, as in the following preparations. The first is specifically for men:

1 saffron crocus before bloom and 1 bean, roasted [probably a fava bean]. Put in oil and anoint the phallus therewith.

This more elaborate one is meant for women:

Crocus from the hills, crocus from the delta, abu-plant from upper Egypt, abu plant from lower Egypt, berry of the uan tree, fresh gruel, linseed, uam seeds, duat plant. Mix all with water and keep moist. Strain before drinking and take for 4 days.

Another diuretic prescribed for children seems quaint at first until it is considered what the ingredients are made from:

Remedy for a child clearing out the accumulation of urine in his body – an old book cooked in oil: smear on his body.

Since old books in Egypt were nothing more than papyrus that must have become like a soft rag when soaked in warm oil, this preparation would have provided the comfort – and probable relief – of a hot-water bottle.

My own personal candidates for quaintest Eber preparations are these two, the first actually a hair dye and the second a treatment for burns, and I would testify in open court that both would most likely be as effective today as they were four thousand years ago:

A hair dye: womb of a cat warmed in oil and mixed with the egg of the gabgu bird.

A cure for burns: Create a mixture of milk of a woman who has borne a male child, gum and ram's hair. While administering this mixture say: Thy son Horus is burnt in the desert. Is there any water there? There is no water. I have water in my mouth and a Nile between my thighs. I have come to extinguish the fire. [To which I will add: Do not get burned without a nursing mother of a son and a man about.]

The problems of teeth and eyes – both somewhat epidemic in ancient Egypt – were treated with saffron, too. The record seems to indicate that tomb painters, working long hours in dark places, relied particularly on ground crocus sprinkled in the eyes to relieve eyestrain. For cataracts, saffron threads were sometimes mixed with some part of a tortoise, usually its brain but in a few instances its shell ground into a fine powder. To strengthen the teeth, the Egyptians followed the recommendations of the old Sumerians and chewed whole crocus bulbs softened in sweet beer. To cure blisters on the gums, a plaster was made from the beer-softened crocus bulb pounded to a paste with incense, cyperus, onions, aloe, and water.

III.

The Minoan civilization ended in a breath. First it was weakened by the things it worshiped – nature and the great sea. Then it was brought down by the progress all nations inevitably make toward their fortune.

Sometime between 1645 and 1500 B.C. (the earlier date is the result of new scientific research, while the later date is the mostly commonly cited), an earthquake shook the nearby volcanic island of Santorini, where years before the Minoans had established two large and prosperous settlements, Thera and Acrotiri. There must have been warning rumblings for some time, because the people had time to abandon the island, perhaps sailing back to Crete, crowding into the coastal cities east of Knossos or the already congested central plains. But these early tremors were also felt on Crete. Palaces and homes in the eastern, central, and southern parts of the island suffered damages. Some of them even collapsed, and their walls along the low-lying seacoast were submerged under a swelling tide.

Priests ran to the shrines to offer prayers and sacrifices to the mother-goddess and her son. As the crisis continued, a human sacrifice was made in at least one shrine, but the ceremony appeared to have been interrupted right after the young noble boy was killed by the sudden collapse of the shrine's roof. Crushed beneath the heavy stone ceiling were the two priests – a man and a woman – and their attendant, whose finger bones still grasped the cup into which the blood of the boy, trussed like a lamb, his throat slashed on the nearby alter, was to have been drained.

But not even this most desperate deed was enough. Soon after the earthquake, the volcano on Santorini exploded. It is believed to have been one of the most powerful natural eruptions the world has ever felt. The entire central part of the island sank, like Atlantis, into the sea, while the lava rushing down the hillsides swallowed whole the streets of Thera and Acrotiri. Loaves of breads left behind in bowls, jugs of wine in storage rooms were preserved in the hot molten stone, while the images of life the inhabitants had painted on their walls – the lily and saffron fields, young boys boxing, a naked fisherman raising high the productive results of his day's labor – were all entombed.

The sun disappeared, and the sky began to rain ash. On Crete, the pearly specks fell in silky drifts across the fertile fields, curling the leaves on the trees, making the rivers turn into a thick gray soup. The ripening crops were all but destroyed; the soil was slowly poisoned. Tidal waves may have washed over the shorelines; harbors slipped beneath the sea.

Knossos, a little away from the epicenter, further up the hillside, was somehow spared. But the country itself was badly shaken. While the palaces and great homes were rebuilt, whole stretches of what had once been arable farmland would have to be abandoned. Worse by far must have been the people's first brush with a shaken sense of the world's balance. What had the Minoans done to anger the gods so much? In this most perfect of worlds, how could they have faltered so badly as to bring down so much wrath? Whoever sat on the throne at Knossos could not answer these questions. Unaccustomed to hardship and embraced by doubt, the island drifted, a wounded, tempting prey.

By 1450 B.C., the Mycenaean Greeks had figured out how to build a fleet of seaworthy boats. They set their stems south and stormed the north and western coasts of Crete, burning and pillaging great palaces and small homes alike. They reduced whole towns to rubble and captured Knossos. When the battles were over, the Minoans found themselves living under a different regime. From our safe distance, it appears as if the Minoans' paintings and pottery lost their whimsical grace and harmony overnight. Women covered their breasts; the flirtatious smile that used to play across their lips disappeared. The men became stiff, their countenance more fierce under the foreign weight of warrior helmets and drawn swords.

The final act is written in the legend of King Minos's search for Daedalus, the fabled sculptor and architect who was given credit for designing Knossos's maze of halls to keep the issue of Queen Pasiphaë's strange passion for a bull in check. When Daedalus was eventually imprisoned in the maze with his son, Icarus, he fashioned feathered wings to bear himself and his son away, thus escaping the wrath of a revengeful king but dooming his imprudent son. Broken-hearted, Daedalus flew on to Sicily, where he was greeted with open arms. There he set to work introducing the artistry of Crete to the Sicilians. Still seeking retribution, King Minos went after Daedalus with his full navy. But Sicily rose up to protect her adopted son, destroyed Crete's legendary navy, and followed Minos home to sack and burn Knossos to the ground.

Egypt prospered for many more years, but the desert, too, finally proved a weak barricade. The later pharaohs spent their time protecting the borders and fending off attacks from one upstart nation after another; eventually divided by feuding nobles, the country grew weak and enervated.

By then, Egypt's cousins from Crete were no more than myths, their once brilliant domain seeming little more than a mirage that a more complicated world could not completely envision. If, however, in its own twilight, Egypt recollected Crete, it must have been with a smile over the pleasures they had known together. They would remind each other of the handsome men with long black hair who had once sailed into the Nile delta, their ships laden with such finely wrought jewelry, with plates and cups and bowls decorated with the most charming designs, the likes of which their children had never seen. The forgotten taste of small black olives and sweet wine would steal across their dry tongues as they lifted their heads and swore a scent they hadn't smelled in ages had somehow come into the room.

"Ah," they would sigh as the mysterious scent filled their hearts with the vaporous image of saffron-clad women waltzing in their flouncing skirts. In the loneliness of their dwindling hours, these old Egyptians would hold themselves still to catch the dimming echo of trilling laughter captured forever within the buried labyrinth.

Travels with the Scholar and the Merchant

It is, in general, tenacious of life.

THEOPHRASTUS, ON THE SAFFRON CROCUS

From the eighth century B.C. to the third century A.D. – the years that span the dawn and dimming of Greece and Rome – the best saffron for perfumes and ointments was gathered in the town of Soli on the coast of Cilicia. The Greek historian Herodotus and the Roman naturalist Pliny the Elder both considered the saffron that grew in the Fertile Crescent to be the most potent in relieving stomach and kidney ailments, but with all the mayhem the Assyrians and Babylonians visited upon one another, it was often too troublesome to get. The Persian variety was suspected of being an aphrodisiac; those who dined with this wily race were frequently warned to be wary, for saffron was stirred into their flavorful dishes for no other reason than to befuddle and weaken the brain. By the sixth century B.C., the intrepid Phoenicians were hawking a new supply that had been planted in Kashmir after Persia invaded it, one whose silky threads had a sharp lusty scent that chased away melancholy and had the profitable characteristic of making a strong, even hardy dye.

The world was shrinking, condensed by colonizing nations, restless kings, and remarkable sailors, and the cacophony of opinions about saffron illustrates the rise of a new shared knowledge. No sooner had the Greeks claimed their superiority in the Aegean than they set sail across the Mediterranean, heading both east and west to settle quite freely along the shores of Asia Minor, the sole of Italy and the southern coast of Sicily. With each journey, they left behind an overcrowded nation and poor rocky soil where grapes and olives grew in abundance, but very little else. It has always been a tantalizingly bothersome question how, in the fifth century B.C., the Greeks became such an astonishingly accomplished race, and it would be much too simple to say that a great deal relied on the abstention imposed by a arid landscape. Yet more than one distinguished thinker has observed that greatness rarely sups with gourmets. The Greeks lived on barley, figs, and wine, the infinite variety of fish from the sea, exceptional honey, and deliciously pungent cheeses made from goat and cow's milk. A proper meal was eaten once a day, after the daily work was complete. And still, when they sat (or, more correctly, reclined) at their table, the Greeks who stayed on the mainland engaged in talking more than feasting, discussing the pleasures of life rather than actually seeking them out. This would explain why Theophrastus, the first great naturalist, could make the very architecture of the tiny saffron crocus, from its long roots to its precious stamen, sound like one of Socrates' more convoluted dialogues. Here is Theophrastus's reiteration of Aristotle's thoughts on the matter of taste and scent:

> *Just as the colors come from the mixture of white and black, so savors come from one of sweet and bitter . . . so the oily is a savor belonging to the sweet, whereas the bitter and salty are about the same, and the pungent, dry-wine astringent and acid come in between. . . . Further, the*

odors must be analogue to the savors. But this is the fact with some: thus there are pungent, sweet, dry-wine, astringent and oily odors, and one could call the decomposing smells analogue to the bitter savors.

This is an interesting and complex point that very neatly ignores the messy role of human nature – of memory and association and the pleasure of the moment, all of which have been known to transform the most bitter flavor into the sweetest nectar. Yet without Theophrastus's observations and the wide arc of his studious rambling, we would not know that fresh saffron lacks its singular potency because the flower is full of water:

Plants and parts with strong odor (and this is the case with the more earthy plants and those where a certain watery power is mixed with the greater earthiness) have a stronger odor when dried and kept for a certain time (and to this group belongs quince and the coronary plants with pungent odours, such as southerwood, especially, sweet marjoram and saffron crocus), for at the same time (1) the wateriness evaporates and the influx of food stops, (2) and some parts at least acquire a concoction of a sort within themselves (which is why the part is more fragrant after removal from the plant).

Theophrastus was of the opinion that cultivation did little for saffron and that in fact it should be subjected to a certain degree of roughness. This was why the wild saffron from Soli, as well as Greece's own variety that grew in its northern region, was best suited for perfumes and ointments: "It likes moreover to be trampled and grows fine when the root is worn down by the tread of feet. This is why the plant is best by the roadside and in well-trampled ground."

The pampered species that was sown in neat rows and received extra helpings of food and water, as it did in Persia and parts of Babylon, were undoubtedly more beautiful to look at. The flowers grew large, in the shape of deep goblets, their violet coloring streaked with a warm red-tinged yellow stripe. But, as Theophrastus observed, doting on saffron was as damaging as coddling a child, for under such soft treatment, with no adversities to strengthen its nature, the character of the flower turned languid, its talents greatly subdued.

Not everyone in Greece, of course, thought as much as Theophrastus did on these matters. The man in the street and especially the woman left forever at home adored saffron just for what it was – a powerful perfume and a pleasing dye. While it grew naturally in the northern regions of the country, there is no record of it being gathered there. Instead, the Greeks were content to pay a pretty penny for the saffron gathered on Crete and Rhodes, and especially for the variety from the land we now call Turkey. It would arrive ready-made in perfumes or ointments, packaged in Egyptian glass vials or the clever little pots the Phoenicians made so well; for dyeing, saffron threads were purchased and stored in clay jars or cloth sacks. Original and artful in so many other ways, the Greeks did not think to find any other uses for saffron – for that they had to travel, separating themselves from the rigors of an austere landscape to fall under the sway of a more fecund order.

It is not that the Greeks became less Greek, but rather they allowed the abundant nature of their adopted land – whether it was Sicily or the coast of northern Africa – to inspire their prodigious natures in more eccentric ways. Plato, for one, was not pleased with such developments and heartily disapproved of what happened to the good Greek soul when it took up residence away from the motherland. With condescending wit, he told his friends that the settlers he had met in Sicily had sunken into "the blissful life." But isn't this what happens when anyone travels? Free of associations, often liberated from obligations and a known past, the traveler experiences a moment of rebirth, when even familiar objects become the focus of infinite wonder when examined under a strange sun.

I saw this once myself when I was much younger, at a time when it seemed I was forever leaving one place and hurrying on to another. As with the Greeks, I was fleeing an overpopulated home, desperate to find success in more promising quarters. The adversities imposed by the rules of a Catholic girlhood do not compare to the glorious precision of ancient Greece, and yet what they do hold in common is a didactic severity in which common desires are pushed aside, ignored if not actively suppressed. If I had been a young Greek woman, forbidden to do much more than to wait for my father to find me a husband, I would have felt the same as I did when, in the company of a school friend who had a working car, I slipped away from my parents' house with little more than a large straw bag filled with clean clothes. It was early in the morning when we drove out of Philadelphia, and by nightfall we were in Maine, close to the Canadian border. By lunch the following day, we were in Nova Scotia, a destination that had been arranged in haste, on little more than a casually mentioned whim, and we were coasting the battered car into a seaside village.

It was the off-season, and all the bed-and-breakfast places were shuttered. The one motel on the outskirts of town was full of what the proprietor called "the boys" – fishermen waiting for the ice in the harbor to break. Since it was the first week in May, the ice had indeed begun to shatter, and most of the boys were out in their boats, but the motel owner still wouldn't give us a room. Instead, he directed us into town to a large Victorian house, its shingles painted a royal purple while the trim on the wide porch that curved around it was the color of an unripe peach. The old woman who greeted us at the door said she could let us have her daughter's room for ten dollars a night, the price including breakfast or lunch. Or, perhaps since it was after lunch, would we care to have dinner with her tonight?

We accepted her invitation and, after paying for one night in advance, went up to our room, where my friend immediately collapsed on one of the small narrow beds covered with a starched pink-flowered organza spread. I tried to follow him in sleep, but I could not. I had never been this far away on my own. There was no thought of family or friends; I felt no sense of guilt about the small untruth I let my parents believe – of being properly chaperoned and closer to home. Instead, I was exhilarated by the sense of being cut off and free to do what I wished in a place where I was a stranger.

I left the house for a walk around the pretty little town, which was situated on a flat plain that spread out behind a rocky shoreline. An old mountain, deteriorated by the wind and sea, shed pebbles onto the curved beach. The fir trees at its top tilted every which way but were clinging on for dear life, their roots sticking out like an old man's bristles from the mountain's red clay face. It was late in the afternoon, and I had the beach all to myself. The sea was absolutely flat, the water in the small bay so still that when I skipped rocks across it, it was possible to believe they went on forever – almost as far as Brittany.

It was, I decided as I wandered up to the wharf and then through the wide streets, the best of towns. Filtered through a chiffon fog, the light turned a delicate iris shade – the kind that when you are young, on your own, and away from everything for the first time, keeps you breathlessly out of doors, feeling that such beauty could beckon only the most magical of nights. A few people were about: men returning from the wharves and heading for a nearby bar, some young boys chasing another boy across a lawn, a woman passing me quickly with a paper bag spilling out bread and vegetables. No one seemed to notice me at all, and I thought of no one but myself, of staking an uncontested claim to these surroundings and prospering in this tangy, savory air.

By the time I returned to the Victorian house, a copiously black night, as iridescent as a raven's back, had settled across the deserted streets. Everyone was indoors; shutters and curtains were drawn across almost every window. I mounted the wide wooden steps of the house, more content than I had been in a long time. My friend and our hostess sat in the softly lit living room and greeted me with confederate smiles as I came in. My friend was a charming man, handsome in his way, though his shoulders were already sloped by the early failure of both a marriage and a teaching career. We had met at a small college attended mostly by people trying to repair their lives. Though I was considerably younger than he was, my own failures were fine companions to his. I liked him very much indeed, and both of us understood each other as friends and nothing more. Yet, as part of my first travel lesson, we were beginning to feel closer to one another in a way that we would never have been if we had stayed in Philadelphia. It was more a familiar sensation than a romantic one, drawn from relying upon one another much more than we would anyone but loved ones back home. Such are the rewards and dangers of traveling: either you come to despise your traveling companions or you adopt them; some have even been known to fall in love and marry.

We were not falling in love, but we were beginning to believe we knew each other to our cores. We sat with our hostess in her properly furnished living room, where the faded wallpaper was covered with strands of ivy growing from two large vases on either side of the mahogany mantelpiece, and I was aching to share with my companion all I had seen. I waited until she finally went off to see to our dinner, and then I described for him everything I had seen. He smiled and nodded, laughed at my narrative where I wanted him to laugh, and smiled wistfully at the things I wished him to regret missing.

In a few minutes we were called into the dining room. A couple of small tables were arranged around the room, used in season when the house was filled with vacationers; for this night, however, we sat down together at the large formal table in the center. It was set with old-fashioned china and a big platter of chicken stew – plain, without much seasoning except for the sweetness of carrots and the fresh butter that melted over the boiled potatoes. There were the last of the winter's supply of root vegetables – mashed turnips and parsnips – biscuits, and a pure white gravy. I ate with genuine enjoyment, shy before our hostess, who decided we must be newly married and in need of some marital wisdom and spoke at great lengths about some of her late husband's peculiar habits. We did not interrupt her or dissuade her, but enjoyed our meal and the stories she told. They made her husband seem to be less gone than just momentarily excused from his vacant seat at the head of the table.

When we had had our fill and helped to bring our empty plates and the serving dishes into the kitchen, she shooed us back to the table for dessert and soon brought out three small bowls, each one filled with blueberries. Between us she set a small pitcher filled with heavy fresh cream. I looked with real dismay at the bowl before me – I did not like blueberries. My mother had bought them often from the local supermarket and sometimes from the farm stands on the side of the road leading to the Jersey shore. My mother liked to bake them into muffins, shortcakes, and pies, and they were the only desserts she made that I would not eat, as I considered them a waste of flour – and all that work! – for such a miserable fruit. I disliked their tartness, the way they popped in my mouth, and when they were baked, how my mother's blueberries turned gummy. Most of all, though I was a contented slovenly child, I despised the stain they left behind on my lips and chin.

The berries in the bowl before me looked even less promising, as small as grit and a darker hue. I would certainly have refused them if I had been anywhere else, but I was touched with a kind of hunger that I had never felt before, and so I poured a good measure of cream into the bowl and spooned some berries into my mouth.

Few things before had ever tasted as delectable as those berries did to me that night. The conversation went on without me; I don't remember raising my head until the bowl was empty. It helped, of course, that the berries were frozen fresh, picked the previous August by our hostess's friend, whose bushes were threatening to break under a bumper crop. I can't with honesty describe what they tasted like – whether they were sweeter or juicier – all I can recall is the pure sense of discovery I felt in their flavor, as unsullied and joyful as a baby's first epicurean adventure. If, in my afternoon of wandering, I had felt a certain sense of proprietary expectation, the berries sealed my desire. After we said goodnight to our hostess and were alone in our frilly room, I told my friend that I wanted to stay in the town. He laughed, thinking I was kidding. But tucked quite modestly in my own twin bed, I firmly held my ground. The next day, after breakfast, I tried to show him what I had seen the day before, but the beach and the wharf, the men in their boats, the kids, the disintegrating mountain, even – and most tellingly – the changing light in the northern sky, did not enchant him. Over more blueberries – this time sprinkled lavishly across a buttermilk biscuit – he insisted we stick to the original plan and leave for Halifax in the morning.

And that is what my friend did, leaving me behind with our perplexed hostess, who mistook my hunger for blueberries as the sign of a broken, instead of an awakening, heart.

Blueberries are a long way from saffron, and the stern coast of Nova Scotia is far from Sicily's clement shores, but the shock of discovering the glories of the familiar in a foreign land are one and the same. When the Greeks arrived in Sicily and built a sleepy little town into the gourmet paradise of Syracuse, they were responding to similar forces. Even with all the markets that the Greek encroachments were opening up and sending back to Athens, nothing compared with the sheer variety of delectable resources Sicily had to offer. In short order, instead of philosophizing about the table, Sicilian Greeks were eating, cooking, writing recipes, and making excursions to distant markets. The most dedicated was Archestratus, a footloose aesthetic who seemed to have traveled to every country bordering the Mediterranean, gathering, tasting, and cooking, then writing his impressions in a long poem, *The Deipnosophists.* The little of it that has survived reveals him to be fearless and creative (though often suffering from an epicurean's tendency to think too highly of himself), willing to try anything at least once, and seeing the possibility of an interesting flavor in the least promising ingredient. He was also something of a purist, admonishing his fellow cooks to practice restraint and not to indulge in the increasingly common and almost always dreadful custom of overwhelming dishes with herbs and spices. He was a sprinkler of ingredients: a sprinkle of salt, a sprinkle of vinegar, and in the one dish of his that survives in which saffron was used – a fish preparation – he instructs that "sprinkling just a little of saffron" will make the dish "like the deadless gods in form and stature."

If Archestratus considered saffron to be worthy of a Greek pot, it was Alexander the Great who inspired its use among the masses. The two men were said to have been friends (as Alexander was also said to have known Theophrastus), and on the bases of Archestratus's travels and his fame as a poet and a cook, Alexander would certainly have gone out of his way to meet with him at least once, perhaps over supper in his campaign tent. Until his father was murdered in 336 B.C., Alexander had been an enthusiastic pupil of Aristotle. He liked to read and discuss great thoughts and considered himself quite knowledgeable on the finer points of life. If his father, Philip, had not (as some say he did) annoyed his wife enough for her to orchestrate his assassination (and if this is indeed true, then she showed an admirable flair for the dramatic by having it staged during a lavish state ceremony with Philip wearing a splendid gold-trimmed white robe), then Alexander might have become a bon vivant. As it was, he fulfilled the role of his father's son and, soon after securing the throne, took off to conquer the world.

Alexander began by crossing the Hellespont, then battling south, and for nine long years he slaughtered his way east through Arabia, Media, and Persia, then over the Himalayas and across the Indus, at which point his weary army would go no farther. He tried to lure them across the Ganges to the fantastic ocean he believed surrounded the world by allowing them to sack nearby towns, to take as their own all the gold and bronze and every fine bolt of silk and linen they could find, but all his men really desired was to return home and be surrounded once more by their own familiar treasures. While Alexander seemed to be blessed with an endlessly ravenous curiosity that would not be satisfied until he saw and touched (and yes, owned) everything the world had to offer, his troops – even his devoted generals – were of a simpler bent. It is not hard to imagine how these haggard souls, burdened with homesickness as well as enormous fatigue must have slumped along the river's soft grassy shores. While slaves prepared for them a feast of local splendor, possibly a goat or lamb newly killed and rubbed with native spices, they were longing for the rough, simple porridge, with perhaps the little indulgences of fennel stirred into it, that accompanied their faded memories of family and friends.

Half of Alexander's men were lucky and were put on boats in the

Indian Ocean for the voyage home; the rest went on foot with him, most of them dying of heat and thirst in the vast deserts south of Persia. Those fortunate few who survived with their leader straggled into Persepolis, the royal city of Persia, and were received, if not with open arms then with the great courtesy and hospitality the Persians have long been known for. It was months before Alexander's men began to feel their strength return, and in that time many had fallen in love with their caretakers. Alexander himself succumbed to the Persians' sumptuous nature. As hard a man as he surely must have been – driven and single-minded, as brutal and decisive as any preying creature is – a corner of Alexander's heart remained susceptible to sensual delights. A year or two past his thirtieth birthday, scarred by the dusty, bloody trail he'd carved through the earth, he was no longer a beautiful youth, and while Alexander would not have admitted it to himself let alone to his companions, he could only have been sick of all the cruelty his great ambition required of him. As sometimes happens when life is led at such a ruthless pitch, the inherent plainness of Alexander's Macedonian nature gave way in a dim hope for absolution, if not of peace, to the voluptuous pleasures of the Persian courts. There was much to delight in, to lose oneself in, for a man who was once taught by Aristotle. By this time in the country's history, Persia had fashioned itself into a sophisticated and cultured nation, with its own celebrated intellects, famous astronomers, and masters of storytelling, poetry, and music. What is more, the way the Persians lived – not only the aristocrats at court but the commoners in town and in the countryside – held great charm. As King Croesus once told the Persian king Cyrus on his way to conquer Greece, all countries would fall to him if they could but experience the "good things on which the Persians lived." Two hundred years later, his prophecy came true as Alexander – the first king of the world – fell under Persia's alluring sway.

For here was a country where a blissful life was truly led, one that was balanced between the heart and the mind, where an amalgamation of tastes drew together to create a sublime and exalted cuisine, and it had long been in place when Alexander settled in. Uncharacteristically, he gave himself up to the country's wines, to the ritual of fine dining. Although he was already wed to the tragic Roxana, he took as his wives the young daughters from each of Persia's two royal clans and ordered his generals and men to marry as well, arranging for this purpose a magnificent wedding ceremony followed by what was known then as a "King's Dinner" that went on for days. At a King's Dinner, the guests were given party favors of gold tiaras to wear and bejeweled gold or silver cups to drink from. They lounged across couches covered with beautiful soft rugs and costly silks arranged in a circle around a great hall and ate their way – sometimes for days on end – through a constant progression of dishes. The set menu for a King's Dinner commenced with finely baked bread and continued on to chicken, duck, doves, and geese all stuffed with spices and surrounded by savory sauces. Then came boar, wild pigs, and such, roasted on long poles, their crisp, glistening skins adorned with rubies and emeralds for their procession around the room before being carved and served. Creatures from the sea were offered next: oysters and scallops in their shells, huge tunas, swordfish, and fat eels. Comely girls danced and performed juggling tricks; musicians serenaded the assembly, and cups were kept topped with wine. More bread was passed, and then there were pastries drenched in honey, peaches and apricots, ripe figs and dates in pomegranate juice, studded with sweet nuts. Perhaps the guests slept on their couches between courses. Surely a few grooms must have pulled their brides into secluded chambers. Even Alexander, who was said to be courtly with women while reserving his true ardor for men, would have felt a sense of duty to his two young wives, and when they returned to the feasting, all would have felt the need for more rejuvenation.

While such sweet interludes must invariably end, their hold on the spirit lingers, and when Alexander and his men finally took their leave of Persia, they left with many things packed into pockets and pouches. The half of his army that sailed straight home from the Ganges would have already regaled their friends and families many times over with the wondrous sights and experiences they had encountered over the nine years they were away; but the souvenirs they brought back with them were likely to have remained only curiosities, things to be hauled out for the telling and then mercifully packed away. But the soldiers returning now with Alexander were another matter. Many of them brought their foreign wives, who in their new home continued to sew their husband's clothes, decorate their new homes, and cook their family's dinners in the manner of their own country, blending together two cultures on a scale that had rarely been seen before. Even the army's beloved leader preferred the style of the Persian kings, and while a bowl of barley may have remained a comfort food for Alexander, the years of living abroad had transformed him into a connoisseur of complicated tastes.

During their sojourn in Persia, both Alexander and his men grew used to sipping saffron in tea and supping on perfumed yellow rice. Alexander's cocktail before dinner was wine mixed with saffron – sometimes alone but at other times with an added dash of myrrh. Some say he kept his golden locks shiny by rinsing his hair with saffron, a well-known beauty treatment used by many at the time. On firmer authority, it is written that Alexander soaked his wound-ridden body in a warm saffron bath, its medicinal benefits easing his stiffened joints and ill-mended cuts. He found this preparation so beneficial that he recommended it to his men, who must have gotten some relief from it because they continued the practice back home in their local baths.

(These saffron baths may have been the original model for Cleopatra's famous soak. Ptolemy, Alexander's favorite general, had stayed with Alexander in Persia and took all of Egypt for himself after Alexander died. Cleopatra, Ptolemy's last descendant, used a saffron bath not for medicinal purposes, but rather as an essential part of her beauty regime. A woman of infinite intelligence but not – as catty contemporaries report – beauty, Cleopatra learned to make the best of what the gods had given her, and in one brief and fragmented tract she was observed to rely on a saffron bath to prepare her body to receive a man – believing that the power of the dissolving threads sensitized her loins, thus heightening her pleasure, as well as her partner's, in the ensuing encounter. A recipe for such a welcoming bath would be composed of about a quarter of a cup of saffron dissolved in enough hot water to cover the body. Soak for as long as the water remains warm. It should be noted that this soak will tint fair skin a light shade of yellow, whereas darker skin tones take on an almost topaz glow.)

The last years of Alexander's life were full of sadness and more wandering, but wherever he went, he brought along his Persian cooks and required merchants to keep him supplied with unusual ingredients. The merchants, in turn, found they could get a better price and even increase demand by simply labeling something as Alexander's favorite, or even the very product that Alexander used. Aegean society had been sophisticated in their taste for quite some time, but as Alexander's endeavors opened up ports and foreign trade, there was now opportunity to distinguish oneself from the neighbors with whatever was rare and exquisite, to become, even by the most tenuous of associations, akin to the exalted few.

And who better than the Phoenicians to supply civilization with its first appointed status symbols? These brave sailors wandered the seas in their wide boats, the only ones not to fear sea monsters or falling off the face of the earth. By race and heritage, they were Semites from Canaan who settled along a spine-thin stretch of land whose ridge of tall mountains made taking to the sea a natural decision. But something personal within them – a tendency to roam, a loner's inclination toward solitary pursuits – impeded the Phoenicians from ever truly uniting into a formal state. What national interest they had centered on commerce, so that Phoenician cities (in what is now known as Lebanon), lorded over by a few families or individual kings, were little more than trading headquarters – established because there was a favorable harbor nearby or because the distance from one town to another was exactly a day's sail. As they opened up trade routes west of Egypt, they established the commanding city of Carthage with a string of smaller settlements along the Libyan and Iberian coasts, where they could restock their boats or beach them to wait out the icy gales that plagued the winter months. After their boats were safely docked, they would find a woman from the native population to warm their beds, then plant a few crops and use these fallow months to mend sails, spin new rope, and make some things to sell in the spring. Skilled carpenters, the Phoenicians' forefathers had built temples for both David and his son Solomon, who later hired more of their kinsmen to make a fleet of ships so he could travel to the legendary gold city of Ophir. The furniture they carved from fine woods and decorated with delicate ivory panels furnished Egyptian and Assyrian palaces. The pots they learned to make from the Minoans and the intricate gold-beaded jewelry they wrought was immensely popular in almost every nation bordering the Mediterranean Sea. All of these things, and whatever they gathered in foraging expeditions, were packed into their boats again, and when the winds once more turned fair and temperate, they took themselves off, plowing both familiar routes and the immense unknown that lay beyond the Pillars of Hercules, their constant travels encouraging allegiance to nothing so much as the cargo they carried.

Rovers are often looked upon with suspicion, distrust, and apprehension; they rub against the grain of hearth and home, and yet half of the strong feelings they engender are caused by envy, the longing we all have to be free of obligations and filial duty and just take off for parts unknown. Such was the way the rest of the world looked upon the Phoenicians, and yet, for many people, they were the only foreigners they would ever meet, the only people to bring news and goods from outside realms. But the interactions – as agreed by both parties – were as brief as possible. (Even during the winter layovers, the Phoenicians seemed to have stayed pretty much to themselves, except of course for the local women they took and then discarded in spring, probably carrying babies in their arms or in their bellies. Given the more than a thousand years they plied the waterways of the western hemisphere, it is not so fanciful to wonder just how many of us have a little Phoenician blood in our veins.)

Herodotus gives a very good account of how a typical selling day went:

> *[The Phoenicians] no sooner arrive – they unload their wares. Having arranged them in an orderly fashion along the beach, leave them and returning aboard their ships, raise a great smoke. The natives, when they see the smoke, come down to the shore – lay out as much gold as they think the goods are worth, then withdraw to a distance. The Carthaginians [as all Phoenicians were called] then come ashore and look. If they think the gold enough, they take it and go their way. If it does not seem sufficient, they go aboard ship once more and wait patiently. Then the*

natives approach and add to their gold until the Carthaginians are content. Neither party deals unfairly by the others: For the Carthaginians never touch the gold until it comes up to the worth of their goods, nor do the natives ever carry off the goods until the gold is taken away.

This was the role the Phoenicians played: their stalwart tubs were roving supermarkets, department stores, purveyors of all kinds of bobbles and trinkets, junk and treasure often mixed together, the sorrowful rankness of human merchandise (for slaves were one of their more lucrative stocks-in-trade) crammed along side the sweetness of rose water.

And many of their ships were packed to the oars with saffron, a particularly prized commodity for them because there were so many uses for it. In almost every port where the Phoenicians dropped anchor, someone would be willing to pay for a bag of saffron. Even on those rare occasions when no specific call for it was found, the clever Phoenicians would still find a way to make a sale, since in their wanderings so many different ways of using the flower had been observed. If, for instance, the perfumers of Rosetta in Egypt happened to be well stocked in saffron when a Phoenician boat pulled in, then they might be asked whether they had heard how the Greeks were making a delicious new honey by feeding their bees on saffron threads. Or if perhaps the quality of the saffron they had picked up in Soli was not up to the needs of the physicians in Gaza, then it could be packed into little pouches hung on leather thongs and their prospective buyers shown how in Rhodes people wore the pouches to the theater so they wouldn't smell their neighbors so much. In such a way, with one call after another, the Phoenicians spread from country to country all the different ways saffron could be used.

For such a pragmatic race, though, one who saw in exploration its capitalistic opportunities rather than its romantic nature, they kept a lot of saffron for themselves. The Phoenicians' pragmatic temperament or their long association with Persia (whom they helped in Persia's disastrous – and ultimately suicidal – campaign against the Greeks) encouraged them to enliven their fish stews with a few saffron threads. They also took to relying on it as a way to produce a cheaper version of their royal purple dye. When dyeing robes for less-than-royal customers, the immense dye works in the Phoenician cities of Tyre and Sidon would dip the cloth once into the purple bath (instead of the usual two or three times) and then overlay the purple with a dip into a saffron bath. The results were not *quite* as deep as an emperor required, but deep enough to satisfy throngs of pretenders.

With so much demand, the saffron fields were picked clean each fall and the bounty sent out across the seas, the exacting labor required for its harvest and production reason enough to charge more for a handful of saffron threads than for a bag of oats. Even in its native countries, the saffron that was once gathered freely in a morning's walk became hard to find and dear to buy. The Phoenicians were merely middlemen, and to cover their costs they sensibly charged their customers more than what their suppliers demanded. They knew that life held too many uses for saffron and that their price would invariably be met.

"The fields so far away, the crop so fragile, the threads so hard to pick, such a small thing, after all, yet look at all the things in life saffron improves!" The Phoenician would remind a reluctant customer as he raked his fingers through the threads in the jar that stood between them, gently releasing the beguiling aroma: *"This comes from Alexander's very fields! He uses more than a jar a day. A full jar! And look at how strong and handsome – like a god – he is. More potent than that you cannot ask for. Why should you not have a little? Is it, after all, not a reasonable price to pay for the modest needs of the likes of us?"*

The seller would smile, take a small amount from the jar, and place it in his customer's hand. The sun could be going down, the tide beginning to rise. There were more markets to travel to, more customers to snag, but these things could not be rushed, and patience must rule. The Phoenician would say no more as he watched his customer slowly give in to the scent rising from his palm. Very soon, a gold coin from yellow-stained fingers would drop into his palm and the two would depart from one another: one filled with needs and anticipations, the other content with an agreeable profit.

The Invading Hordes

I came, I saw, I conquered.

SUETONIUS, *Lives of the Caesars, Julius*

It is a harsh but true culinary fact that nothing is so stimulating to the art of cooking as a good long foreign occupation. Little else accomplishes the savory advances that transpire when one civilization overpowers another. The important ingredient here is time – to have enough of it go by that havoc and despair have lessened, allowing the native and the foreign to slowly seep together in peaceful, though perhaps wary, accord.

This is exactly what happened when the Romans and, many years later, the Moors turned their rapacious natures loose upon the world. The enterprising Phoenicians, being as astute – and good-natured – a commercial society as there ever was, may have seeded the saffron trade up and down the Mediterranean coast. Yet, it was left to these two invaders – different in intent but both with decidedly epicurean bents – to firmly stir saffron into foreign pots.

The Romans were helped in this enterprise by the Greeks, who preceded them in many of the territories they came to control. Until Romans ventured farther into northern Europe, they marched a route –

from the Near East and across northern Africa, from Sicily to the south of France – lined with Greek-planted olive trees and grapevines, the land often inhabited by a native population grown used to foreign rule. First as conquerors and then as slaves sought after as chefs by the rich and famous throughout the Empire, the Greeks left behind traces of their cooking style – their love for the sharpening flavor of vinegar or the brace of lemons, for instance – but the Romans held very firm thoughts of their own on the matter and, along with the unquestioned authority they commanded, were a little more insistent on spreading their love of extravagantly spiced and sauced dishes across their far-flung provinces. In some instances, particularly with regard to some of their favorite fare, the Romans added another ingredient – their fondness for bravado and never-ending controversy.

There hasn't been, and still isn't, a seaside town in all the world – but especially along the Adriatic and Mediterranean Seas – where the inhabitants did *not* concoct some sort of fish soup. Variations from town to town might have been slight, yet they were potent enough that bragging rights and deep slights were uniformly and vehemently broadcast. Nevertheless, between Italy and France – and more specifically between the western coast of Italy and the south of France – there is more than a great similarity – there is kinship. In every important way, bouillabaisse is an ancient French version of the equally ancient Italian (and, to further complicate things and going further back to probably the Greeks) *brodetto*.

In some circles, a statement like this would be considered a fitting excuse for murder, but strong feelings do not change the correlation. Consider for a moment that both dishes call for saffron, which grows wild in parts of Italy and was much adored by the Romans not only for its very real physical qualities but also for the faintly perverse thrill of knowing that a delicate flower was ripped apart just to produce the most meager of quantities. The Romans bathed in it daily and used it to outline their pretty eyes, stirred it in wine as an aperitif, scented their public halls with it, burned it as offerings to gods and goddesses, and strew it in great fragile heaps along parade routes as a small yet unmistakable sign of the country's lavish wealth. And when abroad – no matter whether they were tourists, settlers, or advancing armies – they brought the spice along as one of the necessities of everyday life. This is how it first came to be planted along the southern rim of Gaul. By the time Barbarians invaded Italy in A.D. 271, saffron use in France had declined and in fact was not mentioned there again until the Middle Ages. Depending upon the books you read or the people you are cornered by, saffron returned in the eighth century with the Moors, or the fourteenth century when the papacy took up residence in Avignon.

The people of Marseilles, however, disown any influence – hostile or friendly – but rather claim themselves as the sole creators of bouillabaisse, and thus the first to add saffron to a fishy broth. For proof, they are apt to tell a charming story concerning Venus and how she poured saffron into a fish broth for a very specific purpose. As a dutiful goddess wife, she cooked for her hungry husband, Vulcan, a great big pot of fish soup. She tended her fire carefully, stirred her ingredients with skill. When the soup was finished, Venus presented Vulcan with a large serving bowl, brimming to the top with a sunset-hued broth bursting with many different kinds of small whole fish. Perhaps she also put out a basket of freshly baked bread; certainly (for such a dish demands it) she poured him a generous glass of flavorful wine. Vulcan ate and sipped, and ate some more. When he was finished, he patted his good wife on the head and then, as most husbands are prone to do, stretched himself across a nearby couch for a well-deserved digestive nap. As soon as his deep snoring filled their humble home, Venus abandoned the dishes in the sink and tiptoed out the door into the waiting arms of Mars, her impatient lover. Such was the success of Venus's ruse that each time she wished to see her love, she made the wonderful soup and proved the art in her cunning – for to obtain her heart's desire, she would treat her husband with delicious kindness.

What seems to make this legend a testament to Marseilles's primary role in the creation of bouillabaisse is not the shenanigans of the Roman gods (though in honor of the city's rakish reputation, it would seem to be a logical one), but the claim that saffron is a powerful sedative that many people who have not slept in a Persian bed hold to be a belief peculiar to the French region. Left unsaid is where Venus procured her saffron, for although she was a goddess and, as the story so aptly illustrates, an ingenious one at that, she could not have picked it locally.

No matter. Even without the question of saffron's origin to the region (and, frankly, it seems a good bet to place the first recipe for the soup in the hands of the Greeks who pushed in among the natives first), there are other resemblances between the French and Italian origins of the soups to bolster such a murderous claim as kinship. There is the uniformity in how the soups are made and the strident argument for which types of fish are required to make the most authentic soup. Most recipes call for at least ten different types of fish – most of them small, all of them hard to find anywhere else but in the Mediterranean Sea. A whole afternoon and part of a night can be lost in hungry discord over the subject of whether shellfish, especially lobster, has a place in the broth. But in both countries there is solid agreement over the inclusion of one fish, without which the natives will sniff and haughtily dismiss the offending brew as an inferior impostor. In Italy, the fish is called *scorpena;* in France, it is *rascasse.* Off both coasts, it is a rather ugly specimen with a poisonous spine – not a bad feature for a dish to possess that has often inspired blood feuds.

There are admittedly, however, two explicit differences between the recipes. One of them is small, having to do with a flavoring note that can be easily blamed on regional characteristics. If there is fennel in the broth, it is French; if there is vinegar, it is Italian. Yet both recipes possess a somewhat comparable sharp, edging on tart, flavor that imparts to the soups a variation on a similar theme.

With regard to the other difference, contemplate for a moment the obstinate tendencies of the human heart. A fine bouillabaisse is nothing without the addition of rouille, which is swirled into the soup right before it is served. Rouille is made with sweet and hot peppers, garlic, bread, and olive oil. Everything is pureed together until a thick paste is formed and the intense flavors create a subtle, earthy anchor when added at the last moment to the sea-tinged broth. Since peppers were introduced to Europe with the discovery of the New World, it is safe to say that rouille, in general, is a relatively late addition to Venus's bouillabaisse. Perhaps, the idea behind adding rouille to the old recipe was to distance it further from its foreign heritage. If so, rouille serves the venerable need of the vanquished to affirm a sense of individuality over the conqueror – and in this very individuality creates from the old (and imposed upon) something that is wholly new (and liberating).

In truth, there will always be controversy, always be arguments about the method and lineage of these soups and there is very little hope of putting them to a final rest. Their length and breath will vary from village to village, book to book and even cook to cook with tempered fervor. It is interesting, however, that the arguments have continued into modern times. But they are ultimately enraging, for they tumble in the way of enjoying every perfectly exemplary bouillabaisses and brodetto made far away from a Mediterranean breeze. Wiser folks will avoid the fray and, instead, ponder the delicious evidence of these two old and exalted recipes.

An Ancient Brodetto

1 generous pinch (about a tablespoon, or 30) saffron threads
6 to 8 pounds assorted small, preferably whole, fish, cleaned and gutted
1 pound small squid
assorted heads from sweet-flesh fish (optional)
kosher salt
1 cup olive oil
1 onion, thinly sliced
salt and freshly ground pepper to taste
about 5 cups of water
1¼ cups dry white wine
1 to 2 tablespoons white wine vinegar

Place the saffron in a small bowl and pour over it 3 tablespoons of hot water. Stir and set aside.

At the risk of diving into more controversy, I stand firmly on the side that advises to not spend an unduly amount of time worrying about which fish to choose – or which fish you can or cannot get. Instead, choose a nice selection of both delicate and firm-flesh fish. It is more important that they are whole – or if not whole, that you buy some fish heads to make a good strong broth. An acceptable selection anywhere in the world may consist of cod, rockfish, red snapper, sea and striped bass, sole, monkfish, porgy, and conger eel. Traditionally, this soup is served with the fish left whole. Although this adds considerable strength to the broth and drama to the presentation, whole fish make a mess in a soup bowl and are treacherous to people with a phobia for bones. Consider using fillets instead and compensating in the broth with a few more fish heads. If you still want to try whole fish, remove all the bones with needle-nose pliers.

Once you have resolved this question, proceed to make the broth as follows:

Clean the fish and cut the larger ones into even-sized pieces. Remove the ink-sac, eyes, and cuttlebone from the squid and cut it into strips. Wash all the fish carefully in plenty of salted water. In a large, heavy stockpot, warm the oil over medium heat and sauté the onion gently until golden. Add the squid and the saffron and continue to cook, stirring gently. When the squid has turned yellow, season with salt and pepper. Add any fish heads you have bought for the stock and pour in the water – add more if needed to cover all the fish. Bring to a boil, then lower to a simmer and cook for 30 minutes. Remove the fish heads from the stock. You may strain the stock if you wish, but you want to reserve the squid for the soup.

In the bottom of another large stockpot, place the firmer-flesh fish. Layer on top the more delicate-flesh fish, and then pour in the stock with the pieces of squid. Mix the wine and the vinegar together and pour into the pot. You may have to add a little more hot water to completely cover the fish. Bring to a brisk boil and cook uncovered for 15 minutes, or until the fish is tender. Shake the pot from time to time so the fish on the bottom don't stick. Taste the broth and correct the seasoning. Serve with fried or toasted bread. Serves 6.

An Ancient Bouillabaisse

1 generous pinch (about a tablespoon) saffron threads
6 to 8 pounds assorted small, preferably whole, fish, cleaned and gutted
1 pound small squid
½ cup olive oil
assorted heads from sweet-flesh fish (optional)
kosher salt
3 cloves garlic, chopped
1 small fennel bulb, chopped
1 onion, thinly sliced
sprig of thyme
1 bay leaf
zest from 1 small lemon
about 5 cups of water
8 medium tomatoes, peeled, seeded and chopped
1¼ cups dry white wine

For the rouille:

2 red bell peppers, grilled or roasted, skin charred and removed

2 hot red peppers, seeded and finely chopped

3 garlic cloves, chopped

1 teaspoon kosher salt

3 baguette slices (about 1 inch each), crust removed

½ cup extra-virgin olive oil

Place the saffron in a small bowl and pour over it 3 tablespoons of hot water. Stir and set aside. The same note concerning the fish selection related in the brodetto recipe applies equally here.

Proceed to make the fish stock: In a large stockpot, heat the olive oil and add the squid, fish heads, salt, garlic, fennel, onion, thyme, bay leaf, and lemon zest. Cook over medium heat until the squid, onion, and garlic are golden. Add water and bring to a slow simmer. Continue cooking, uncovered, for about 20 minutes. Strain the stock through a fine-meshed strainer and discard the vegetables and fish heads (you can pick out the squid and reserve it for the soup if you wish).

Wipe out the stockpot and layer the firmer-flesh fish on the bottom, then the more delicate fish on top. Sprinkle the tomatoes over the top layer of fish. Pour the saffron brew over the fish; then add the fish stock and wine. Bring to a simmer and cook for 10 to 15 minutes or until the fish is cooked through.

To prepare the rouille:

Cut the roasted red bell peppers in half; remove the seeds and stem and then coarsely chop. In a blender or a food processor fitted with a metal blade, puree the pepper with the hot peppers, garlic, and salt for about 1 minute, or until smooth. Scrape the sides of the bowl down.

Soak the bread slices for a minute in a little warm water. Squeeze out the excess water, add the bread to the pepper mixture, and pulse a few times to mix. Transfer to a bowl. Slowly add the olive oil, stirring with a wooden spoon to make a fairly smooth paste.

You may stir the rouille directly into the soup right before serving, but traditionally it is served alongside so that guests may add whatever amount they wish. Serves 6.

What a dark and awful time it was when, from the fifth to the sixth century, the Barbarians descended from the north and east to sweep the dust of the Roman Empire away! Out went everything, everything that gave ordinary life its sweetness: music and art and saffron. In his wonderfully readable dictionary, *Food: An Authoritative and Visual History and Dictionary of the Foods of the World* (New York: Simon & Schuster, 1980), Waverley Root describes this time best: "The use of saffron is only imaginable in a refined society. . . . The harsh, coarse, belligerent society which succeeded the Roman Empire could not be bothered. Where were the customers to pay for the fastidious work of picking stigmas out of flowers to prettify unsubtle food?"

Spices in general were lost on the Barbarian tribes, but a spice as labor-intensive, as poetically lovely as saffron didn't stand a chance. For several hundred years, one could travel the length and breadth of Europe and not find a single pinch of saffron – not even a crocus blooming on the edge of an autumn field. Throughout all of the once-sophisticated realms of the Roman Empire hardly a soul remained who could remember the addictive allure or the earthy pleasure of saffron's sharp scent.

Therefore great praise should be lavished upon the Moors – and a sigh of relief offered that they cast their acquisitive eyes north and west. In the early years of the eighth century, after three hundred years of marauding Celts, Visigoths, Saxons, and Huns, the Moors raised the long sword of Muhammad and swarmed with religious zeal up the boot of Italy and through the Pillars of Hercules. In their formidable wake, the lamp of civilizing enlightenment was once more raised. French tradition has it that in A.D. 732, when the Moors were stopped at Poitier by the great Charles Martel, they lingered long enough to plant a few saffron corms, thereby reintroducing the spice to France before they did so anywhere else. The account may be true, but recalling that these are the same storytellers who presented Venus and her soup as gospel truth, it should be viewed with a tiny wink at the very least. The Moors were many things – scholars and poets and gourmets – but it cannot be forgotten what seasoned and aggressive warriors they were – warriors, no less, who were on a divine mission to bring the Muslim religion to Christian infidels. No matter how much they may have craved a delectable meal, it is hard to imagine that they would stop in midbattle to prepare a saffron field.

Even in the comparative peacefulness of their eventual conquest of Spain (comparative because there never was a time when they weren't battling the Christian kings in the northern provinces and rival leaders among their own sects), it took another two hundred years before the Moors got around to planting a decent saffron crop in the central and southern provinces of Andalusia, La Mancha, Valencia, and Castile. By the end of the tenth century, the Moors' occupation had made Spain the center of power and culture in Europe. They established magnificent universities where science, literature, and philosophy flourished, and they created beautiful sun-drenched cities filled with lovely public buildings and mosques. In the countryside, they built intricate irrigation canals that made the dusty parched plains bloom with orchards, vineyards, and vegetable farms.

It is easy to see why the Moors held on to the southern part of Spain for as long as they could – fighting for it even after their fortunes had turned. What they saw in it remains today, the land rippling with a brilliant voluptuousness. In summer, the heat is thick, the air swollen with shattering sunlight. Flowers bloom in hot colors – deep reds and yellows and orange – growing in dense profusion. It is a perfect land for growing saffron and – once the irrigation canals flooded the lowlands – rice. When tender green shoots of young rice plants first sprouted above the shallow glassy water fields and damson-tipped crocuses cracked open the hard brown soil, the Moors must have looked upon their handiwork and smiled at the heaven they had created on earth.

The type of food that developed in this part of the country is much lighter than that of the rest of Spain – partially because of the intense climate (it is hard indeed to eat rich, heavy meals under the torpid heat of the southern skies) and partially because of the lingering influence of the Moorish occupation. The flavors are distinct, sensually aromatic, using citrus and woody accents such as cinnamon and clove. Some spiciness may be introduced, but more likely sweetness – of almonds and honey.

Above all, there are rice dishes. The kinds of rice the Moors introduced, short and medium grain, is still grown today in the region. Unlike long-grain varieties, these types soak up flavors and remain a little chewy. Once introduced to the grain, the general population found rice to be easy to grow, filling, and versatile, and it quickly became an important stable of the local diet.

By far the best-known Spanish rice dish is paella, and it has nearly as many hard and fast rules as brodetto and bouillabaisse. It is a slightly younger dish but conceived with ancient roots. The Moors did not introduce paella, yet without their culinary influence and their gifts of saffron and rice, it would never have been created. After a long day of work or study, the Moors gathered outdoors to enjoy the soft breezes and the company of friends and family. A cooking fire would be started, the evening meal prepared, and in a slow and leisurely manner the day drew to a sweet, delicious end.

A true paella is primarily a rice dish. The cooking vessel it is made in is responsible for some confusion surrounding the dish; although many dishes may be cooked in a paella pan, it is generally recognized that there is only one traditional paella recipe, and that is the one from Valencia, where the dish is thought to have originated. The most common cooking method is indeed reminiscent of Moorish customs, but it also relates to the habit of farmhands working in the region's orchards and fields. The ingredients consist of what can be easily found: a chicken that wandered fortuitously from the coop and a rabbit luckily snared in a trap; snails that creep their way through marsh grass; broad beans and lima beans, an onion, and garlic pulled from the vegetable garden. A little envelope where saffron is kept is retrieved from a pocket. Small bottles of white wine and olive oil are pulled from a pouch. Some twigs, trimmings from a nearby grapevine perhaps, are piled together for a small fire; the flat, wide pan is wiped clean and placed on top of the flames. Quickly – in twenty minutes at the most – the meal is assembled, stirred, and simmered. Everyone gathers around the pan and fills their growling bellies with the delicious results.

Variations of this simple recipe probably materialized quickly, though the one that most people in the world today think of as paella was created only recently. That recipe is chock-full of seafood and possibly chorizos – spicy Spanish sausage. Other recipes call for squid ink (which makes the dish black instead of yellow), and nothing but vegetables. There is even an all-seafood variety that is served like bouillabaisse with an added little paste (an aioli) mixed in at the last moment.

Each of these variations is wonderful in its own way. All of them are cooked in the tradition of paella, using a paella pan. But I will record here what is essentially the parent recipe. You will need to gather together four things to begin: short- or medium-grain rice, saffron, a paella pan, and a wood-burning fire (a charcoal grill will suffice, but it is really worth the risk of breaking local fire ordinances and annoying the neighbors to clear a little spot in the backyard, rim it with flat stones, and build a little teepee of ten to twenty pieces of dry wood).

Paella Valenciana

2 pinches saffron threads
1 cup fresh lima beans
4½ cups water
⅔ cup olive oil
1½ pound chicken,
cut into serving pieces
1 pound rabbit,
cut into serving pieces
5 cloves garlic, chopped
1 medium onion, chopped
1 cup green beans, trimmed and
halved
1 tomato, peeled and finely chopped
2 teaspoons paprika
salt to taste
12 small land snails
2½ cups short-grain rice

Build a small fire outdoors. Place the saffron in a small cup and add 3 tablespoons of warm water. Stir and set aside. Meanwhile, on a stove, place the lima beans in a medium-sized saucepan with 2 cups of the water. Bring to a boil; lower to a simmer and cook until just tender.

Place the paella pan directly on the fire. Heat the oil in the pan and fry the chicken and rabbit pieces until nicely brown. Remove the meat to a plate and reserve. Add the garlic and onion directly to the pan. Stir and cook until the onions are translucent. Add the green beans and gently fry. Add the tomato, paprika, and salt and mix to blend. Add the lima beans and their cooking water and stir everything together. Move the paella pan to the side of the fire where it is not very hot. Return the meat to the pan. Blend everything together with one or two stirs and let cook for about 30 minutes or until the meat is cooked through.

Add the snails and stir in the saffron. Move the pan back to the center of the fire and add the rice, spreading it out as evenly as possible underneath all the ingredients. Pour in the rest of the water. Let cook for about 10 minutes undisturbed. Then taste the rice to see if it is done. It should be soft on the outside but quite firm on the inside.

Remove the paella pan from the heat and allow the rice to rest for five minutes before serving. Serve directly from the pan. Serves 6.

As is the case with brodetto and bouillabaisse, it is hard to make paella for only a few. All of these dishes are social events, meant to be savored for both their individual parts and their magnificent whole. They are feasts in every possible way – of abundance and flavor and gracious fellowship. And in their sunny saffron guise, they are survivors of a time when the world was infinitely more conquerable.

For God and King

Swevenes engendren of replecciouns.

[Dreams are born of gourmandizing.]

CHAUCER, *The Nun's Priest's Tale*

Have you ever stumbled from the deep woods after a long camping trip? Even if there were provisions enough, they were, at best, rudimentary – an unadorned shelter, something to keep you warm, food plainly and quickly cooked over an open flame – sufficient to endure but not enough to inspire. Unkempt, nearly feral, ignorant of all that has gone on in the wide world, you lurch back into civilization saturated with a profound hunger for small luxuries – a soft bed, a warm bath, the layered seasons of a flavorful meal, all the elementary desires that have stoked the best of human vision.

Think of the Dark Ages as the longest, most chaotic camping trip that anyone has ever been on; by the time the world staggered from the Barbarian thicket into the Middle Ages, it was more than ready for a little respite. The trouble was, most everything of indulgent lightness and amusement had gone with the Romans. The feudal lords in their cold stone towers were only a little better off than the peasants they fed and protected. The good priests and nuns behind their thick cloistered walls fared better, if only because they had rescued the Romans' libraries. From Theophrastus and Aristotle they learned how to explore nature and the universe; from Herodotus and Pliny they took to heart the lessons of history. And while they preached the blessings of abstinence and their flock gnawed on marrow bones three days a week, these wise men and women turned to their shelves and found the cookbook written by the Roman Apricus before (as some say) he killed himself over the fortune he wasted on fine food. In his exacting book, the religious orders found ways to season their eggs and legumes with delectable herbs and even to disguise them into the shape of savory rump roasts.

It was the Lord – or rather, his Chalice, the vision of it blazing across the sky for everyone to heed – that in A.D. 1095 led the masses completely from the woods into the center of all the splendor the world held at the time. Their religious fervor should not be questioned, but for the young men (and a few of their sisters and an old father or two) there surely was the giddy thrill of striking off on an adventure – to be doing *anything* else but merely scratching out a living surrounded by the same old faces in the same old countryside. This eager army of untried soldiers, wearing chafing homespun emblazoned with a crimson cross, tramped behind their liege lords, who were dressed in their finest clanging armor, confident that they would quickly slay the backward infidels who held captive the Holy Land where Christ had walked. So that when they at last arrived in the Byzantine court, where the remnants of Rome and even a few tattered threads of ancient Greece remained, they were hardly prepared for the majestic empire spread before their drawn swords, one whose very existence tempted their God-fearing souls by filling their hearts and minds with strange and unaccustomed lusts.

For here the crusaders discovered the cool slide of iridescent silk on bare skin, the furry opulence buried in the folds of royal purple velvet, gold and silver covered with priceless gems, and a rich variety of scents – enticing and narcotic, their odor heightened under a blazing sun. These fine Christian warriors on their first Crusade, more innocent than Alexander's army ever was, were babes awakening to pure pleasure. Seduced by coffee, by turmeric, by lotus oil, by the luminous quality of lightly veiled dusky skin – before such fascinations only the most devout and single-minded knight would have stayed his course through the siege of Antioch and Tripoli to Jerusalem's walls and sailed back home untouched. Many, indeed, were forever bewitched and remained to raise olive-skinned children with flaxen hair on tales of cold-swept northern kingdoms.

But those who did at last return came back like every soldier from a foreign war, with pockets splitting from the weight of exotic and curious treasures. In the hollowed-out hilt of their battered swords, secreted in the folds of frayed tunics and rusty, dented armor, they carried trinkets they had grown fond of, roots and seeds that made their broths and stews taste better, powders that, when stirred into their coarse wines and ales, turned them into sublime and potent elixirs.

The women who greeted their long-lost men were just as ravenous for something new – and probably more so for the years they had been left behind. After a few lessons from their weary men, they set to thinking of all the ways these new ingredients could enhance their lives. It must have been an awakening of the sweetest rapture to have their tasteless porridge turn suddenly vibrant from the addition of just a little cinnamon sprinkled across the top, or the evening's thin cabbage soup become nearly succulent with the inclusion of a mash of almonds and ginger. The pity, though, was that for many lowly soldiers, what was stolen home would have been the last of such treasures they ever possessed in their brief lifetime. For although this first Crusade renewed the old trade routes and wondrous goods began to appear in even the most remote village markets, by and large it was only the lords and ladies who could afford the stiff price the merchants took to charging for such wondrous stuff.

Medieval traders did not have Phoenician sailors to ply the tricky Mediterranean currents, and rather than run the risk of losing their investments to sudden squalls, they preferred to bring their precious cargo the long way, across central Asia, over the craggy mountains of eastern Europe, for the short voyage across the relatively tame waters of the Adriatic into northern Italy. Every step of the way brought demands for compensation – from the growers, of course, but also from anyone else who touched the shipment, if only to transfer sacks from camel to donkey, to wooden cart. The Italian merchants who bought the shipments used linen from Germany to wrap the spices in, then paid for local tanners to fashion sturdy leather pouches in which to ship the bundles to the principalities of France, Germany, and England. For these reasons alone, by the time a pound of spice was put up for sale, its price was more than double what it had been when its journey began. It's no wonder, then, that when the lady of the house came home from market with her basket full of precious pepper, ginger, cinnamon, and cumin, she did not store them in the kitchen with the other provisions but instead turned to her private chambers and locked them up in the wardrobe where the furs and fancy robes were kept, and doled the spices out, pinch by pinch as they were needed, to her cook.

Yet expense was more than half of the attraction to the nobles who clamored after these tasty gems. At a time when so few outward signs of power and wealth were available, when feudal folk lived and ate and even slept together in close proximity, what better way was there to demonstrate earthly worth than to be able to present a banquet filled with costly spices? The main diversion of the day was the evening's meal, and feasts were set up on the slightest pretense. Both went on for hours and – especially in the biggest households – with elaborate pomp and procedure. The dining hall became the heart of the castle, and the kitchen – no longer a mean corner of a muddy yard, but a spacious room unto itself – proceeded to turn out new dishes robed in thick sauces ever more bejeweled in copious layers of the world's most flavorful ingredients.

And of all the spices the nobles procured, none were held in as high esteem or merited as much prestige as saffron; such was its place of honor that it did not need an arduous journey nor even an exotic origin (though certainly it had that) to command exorbitant sums. Of all the spices that came out of the East, only saffron successfully took to European soil. People in Cornwall still credit the Phoenicians for leaving behind some saffron bulbs. There were the fields the Moors planted in nearby Spain and the patches they were said to have sown in Poitiers in the kingdom of Aquitaine. Farther south in France, an especially good supply grew in Albi in the Languedoc region, not to mention the crocuses the Greeks and Romans once cultivated in Provence, which by then had naturalized and were growing in wild profusion among the sun-bleached rocks above the Mediterranean. Italy, too, had a fine supply; the citizens of Florence even embroidered the crocus blossom on the city's coat of arms and year after year annoyed their Sicilian cousins by asserting that the most potent harvest was that from Florence.

The ponderous labor so famously required to gather one good measure of saffron was also not at issue in its fee, for nearly everything that sustained life – let alone that which simply gave delight – involved an equal amount of enormous labor. What made saffron so dear and worth so much in the minds of status-seeking nobles was its shimmering alchemy, how its crumbling auburn threads stained everything they touched a golden hue and, in so doing, announced to all who sat about the table the host's unquestioning fortune.

This alchemy was called *endoring* and was really nothing more than food coloring, but in an age enthralled by transformations of every kind, when Ovid's tales of metamorphosis were revised with great delight, the process was used not only to change base into rare, but also to transform the ordinary into the fantastical. Here, from a translation of the great medieval French cookbook *Viandier* by Taillevent, edited by Terence Scully (University of Ottawa Press, 1988), is a recipe that fulfills both desires:

A Golden Swan (Cigne Resvestu)

Take the swan and inflate it between its shoulders as with stuffed poultry and slit it along its belly. Then remove the skin together with the neck cut off at the shoulders and with the legs remaining attached to the body; then fix it on a spit, interlarded as poultry, and glaze it with saffron; and when it is cooked, it should be redressed in its skin, with the neck either straight or flat. Endore the feathers and head with a paste made of egg yolks mixed with saffron and honey. It should be eaten with poivre jaunet.

Yellow Pepper Sauce (Poivre Jaunet)

Grind ginger, long pepper [see page 88 for description], saffron – and some people add clove with a little verjuice [a little like vinegar, made from fruit, particularly acidic berries] – and toast crumbs; infuse this in vinegar and boil it when you are about to serve the meat.

What a sight this Midas swan must have made as it was paraded about the dining hall on a great platter for all to see before being presented to the host and the honored guests! Many other creatures were adorned in the same golden robes – peacocks with their plumes erect and fanned, porpoises curled in a leaping arc, boars with their tusks buffed to a high sheen, and a truly fantastical creature that united the head of a chicken with the trunk of a pig. Apples, cakes, and pies all turned golden – as well as rounds of thick heavy bread that were used for plates because crockery was difficult to mass-produce. By banquet's end, the bread would be embedded with bits of charred meat and thoroughly soaked with sauces and gravies. Sometimes the bread plates were collected to give to the poor who waited at the castle door for what would truly be a delicious beggar's treat. Other times guests would wrap the weighty, dripping rounds in a square of linen and take it home with them, saving it for the next day's breakfast in a dish that was known as sops.

Other colors were used for endoring – parsley for green, berries for red – but the finest tables and the most important feasts were covered in dishes painted gold with saffron. In another type of gilding, the monks in their monasteries hoarded saffron to mix with iron mordant for the gold paint they used to glorify God and the saints in illuminated manuscripts. A nameless scribe paused in his solitary devotion to write down a prescription for the paint: "Take pure tin finely scraped, melt it and wash it and apply it with glue upon letters or others places you wish to ornament with gold. When you have polished it with a tooth, take saffron, moisten with the white of an egg and when it has stood a night, cover with a brush the places you wish to guild."

When saffron did not glitter, it joined all of the other spices and was thrown into a bubbling cauldron or smeared across a flank of meat. Of the 116 recipes that make up another famous cookbook of the period – the *Forme of Curye,* which was compiled in 1390 by the chefs of England's Richard II – nearly half contain saffron – along with pepper, ginger, cloves, cinnamon, cumin, and mace. None of these recipes give quantities, and there is no reason to suspect that any of the spices were added more heavily than the others but were instead guided by the judgment – and fondness – of individual chefs. With such a jumble, though, one flavor would be hard to distinguish from another, and the results would be (and are, if you ever draw the courage to try your hand at one of these recipes) an exacerbation of flavor. And that was probably the point: after so many years of a bland subsistence diet, medieval recipes are testimonies to discovery run amok, with ingredients added simply because they *could* be added, without much thought given to whether they *should* be there at all. People came to the feudal table not so much to taste what they ate but to experience the tasting. While the Crusades renewed interest in travel, and the Moorish conquests put the Continent in close contact with the erudition and elegance of the East, Europeans of this period were very much arrivistes, longing for delectable sophistication yet much too hungry to accomplish it with finesse or discernment.

Of course, many in the medieval world would have argued this point, those who considered themselves already evolved and extremely cosmopolitan. One who wrote quite stringently of his refinement is known to us as the Goodman of Paris because he left behind a little book entitled *Le Menagier de Paris* (1393), which is filled with instructions for his new bride on how to run a cultivated and proper household. He was seventy-five years old, a well-to-do bourgeois with a large house in Paris; she was fifteen, an orphan from a good country family whose marriage had been arranged by the uncle who had taken her in when her parents died. The Goodman considered her a perfect wife – with some wealth of her own to bring to the marriage, pretty in form and face and unschooled (and therefore virtuous) in the ways of the world. In his book, he sought to mold her into a polished companion for his old age; though mindful that there was a good chance she would outlive him and take another husband, he strove to make certain that she would take care of his good name and fortune. He guides her in everything – from the hours to say her prayers, to the vexing problem of how to rid the house of fleas, to the proper – and exact – way she should receive her husband at night:

Be loving and intimate with your husband for he is her beginning. I pray you to bewitch and bewitch again the husband whom you will have. Mind that in winter he has a good fire without smoke and that he is well couched and covered between your breasts and there bewitch him.

He even copies for her his favorite recipes:

Take your chickens and cut their throats. Scald them and pluck them, being careful not to tear their skin. Parboil them. Take a tube, push it between the skin and the flesh and blow the chicken up. Cut it between the two shoulders, without making too large a hole, and pull out the innards, leaving the thighs, wings, neck with all the head and feet with the skin.

To make the stuffing, take mutton, veal, pork and the dark meat of the chicken, all raw, and chop them up. Pound them in a mortar with raw eggs, good rich cheese, good spice powder [generally a mixture of pepper and ginger and either a combination of hot spices – powdor fort *– or sweet spices –* powdor douce*], a little saffron, and salt to taste. Fill the chicken and truss the hole. With what is left of the stuffing, make balls like little lumps of woad and cook them in beef broth or boiling beef water with plenty of saffron. Don't boil them too hard or they will fall apart. Then put them on a very thin spit and glaze them with a great many egg yolks beaten up with a little saffron. If you want green glaze, bray greens, then well-beaten egg yolks, and run them through a strainer for greens.*

With this, glaze the chicken when it is cooked and the balls as well, holding your spit in the pot with the glaze and throwing the glaze all along it. Put the spit back on the fire two or three times, so that your glaze will stick. Be careful not to let the glaze get too close to the fire or it will burn. (Tania Bayard, ed. and trans., *Ménagier de Paris* [HarperCollins, 1991])

Nothing remains behind to tell us how the union worked out, though between the Goodman's words there are hints that, even as he wrote his book, his wife appeared restless, or at least unsatisfied, a predicament that is not so unusual when a child is coupled with a grandfather. But this was a common arrangement throughout the Middle Ages, and from such tortured situations arose the medieval ideal of chivalry and courtly love. The plot of a thousand troubadour songs and verses were launched from the furtive glances of the young wife toward a bold young man who would risk the deadly fury of the older – and more powerful – husband to possess her. A woman in medieval times was little more than property belonging to the men in the family, and time and again she proved a useful commodity in a voluble economy in which one's station could be changed with little more than the mumbled words of the marriage vows. Even the most powerful women of the time – Eleanor of Aquitaine and her granddaughter Eleanor of Castile, for instance – had little to say over their marital fate. Only the poor could afford to marry for love; the best that could happen in a family of means was for a boy and girl to be united as children and then grow up together to be, if not romantically in love, then at the very least fond of one another. In such an atmosphere, old men had reason to worry about wandering wives. Those tales the court poets recited at banquets of brave knights fighting for their queens, risking life and limb for a mere token of their affection, of beautiful maidens threatened by dragons, locked in towers, and stolen by marauding rival kingdoms only fanned forbidden desire, and the prospect of steep punishment (men often got away with adultery, whereas women were routinely put to death for it) merely made the game of wooing and flirting that much more exhilarating.

The Goodman of Paris dealt with his insecurities with a common prescription. After warning his wife of the dangers of fast friends and young men who would do her harm, he gives instructions for making a brew called Hypocras, a mixture of wine and spices with an ancient lineage stretching back to the long-buried Sumerians that was poured at the end of every banquet for a final farewell toast – and every night in the privacy of the home to give men "courage" for the night's labor. This particular recipe is recorded in Madeleine Pelner Cosman's *Fabulous Feasts: Medieval Cookery and Ceremony* (G. Braziller, 1976):

Hypocras

To red or white wine add cinnamon, ginger, a penny's worth of spikenard of Spain, saffron, cloves, long pepper, nutmeg, marjoram, cardamom and grains of paradise. Let steep a good long while, then strain the wine and serve.

Now turn to regard the Goodman's wife – a girl who most likely grew up listening to the wisdom and beliefs of a countryside still steeped in the magic of a more heathen age. She, perhaps, had knowledge of another brew. If she was as good and virtuous as the Goodman thought, she would travel in the month of June to the fields beyond Paris's walls and gather *langdebeef* leaves. Then she would bring them home and steep them in a gentle broth, and whenever she felt her husband's attention wandering away from her, she would give him the broth to sip and thus bring his heart back to her.

Or if, in time, *her* attention turned elsewhere, she would pull down the ingredients for this magic elixir:

A Love Potion

Take thick spring honey and add enough saffron to make it as darkly red as blood; then at its center press a clove and roll the ball in a powder of cinnamon, nutmeg and pepper and give it to the one you would have love you.

The honey ball must be held in the beloved's mouth to dissolve slowly, sweet and burning across his tongue, and by the time the last of the honey slipped down his throat, he would look upon the Goodman's wife with yielding love.

The Red Bodice of the Middle Ages

It is hard to read accounts of medieval banquets and not wish that you could be a part of it – to partake of such outlandish food and drink in the midst of all the fanfare and extravagance that made up even the simplest meal. The only place today where such a meal can be had on anything like a regular basis is probably in the homes and meeting rooms of the Society for Creative Anachronism.

The members of the society are hell-bent on recreating an idyllic interpretation of the years before A.D. 1600, with particular devotion given to the period of the High Middle Ages (the fourteenth and fifteenth centuries). The medieval world of the society is never stricken with the Black Death, and no one is in danger of being burned at the stake. At the wars the society stages each summer, limbs don't gets hacked off and heads are rarely bashed open (though occasionally, in the heat of play, mistakes and accidents occur, and then full advantage is taken of the nearest modern medical facility). Though there are tales of feuds and quarrels in the society's history, none of the currently sixteen kingdoms ever invade one another. (Most of these kingdoms are within the United States, where the society was founded in

1966 – but others are located in such far-flung countries as Antarctica, the Middle East, and Africa, places where normally you would not expect to find a single soul nostalgic for medieval European pageantry.) Although the kingdoms are ruled by kings and queens, they are chosen not by divinity or by might, but rather incongruously along democratic lines.

There is, in short, nothing remotely *medieval* about the Creative Anachronists' domain. Men and women (and their children, if they have them) who seem to thrive quite nicely in the twenty-first century as computer programmers, lawyers, artists, stock traders, investment bankers, secretaries, store clerks, teachers, bureaucrats, civil service employees, postal workers, and (for some reason) a fair representation from the United States Coast Guard, go home at night and on weekends and become Lord this and Lady that – Dame Edith of Hedgerow; the Count of Maulvania; Moirdrid, the serving wench; Dafydd, the smithy of Hayland.

To really get an idea of the passion that imbues the society's members, spend some time on the Web, cruising all the sites the individual kingdoms and members have put up. These may be people with one foot in the past, but they are head-over-heels in love with cutting-edge computer technology. Some sites are interactive, and others have a rich audio component; all of them come with graphics, whereas the simplest site is composed of a meticulously (verging on nit-picking) researched and lengthy manuscript concerning some arcane topic relating to the period. One quick scan through the cooking sites, for instance, will leave you with the impression that no one else in the world could possibly be cooking with as much scrutiny as the society's members. Arguments are raised about everything: a simple query about long pepper and grain of paradise – two admittedly unfamiliar spices, the first one in the pepper family and the other a fiery little berry from

Ghana – elicit over forty rather heated responses of minute detail concerning the hows, whens, wheres, and even what the spices are. One entry reads as follows:

> *Greetings: I must say I am sorry to say that the other gentleman who posted information on this topic is sorely misinformed. . . . Graine de paradis . . . is now known as Grains of Paradise or Melegueta pepper (*Aframomum melegueta*) and is related to cardamom (*Elettaria cardamomun*) and ginger (*Zingiber officinale*). They are all members of the genus* Zingiberaceae.
>
> *Long pepper is just that . . . known as Indian long pepper, Jaborandi pepper, or Roman long pepper (*Piper longum*). I have been looking for a source for it and as of yet have not received any, though I continue to look. You might want to try Cubebs . . . or tailed pepper . . . (*Piper cubeba*), also known and used in period. . . . They have a unique taste that is hard to describe, but wonderful.*
>
> *– Lord Xaviar the Eccentric*

Equally passionate dialogues concern anything remotely connected to the period (so long as it is pleasant – remember, no plagues), as well as a fair amount of interkingdom taunts and jeering – especially after a war, such as the Pennsic War held each summer by the eastern kingdoms. Styles of armor – the cut of a helmet, the quality of the opponent's chain mail – and dress; who wore modern underwear and who was seen with a cooler in their campsite are all laid open and subject to ridicule in the service of becoming – to the very last detail – a genuine Creative Anachronist.

Many I know would find this all strange – even creepy – and yet for a long time I was actually deeply intrigued by the society. I had passed my thirtieth birthday and felt that I was flying across the line that divides youth from age. I'm sure there was also a deep sense lurking around somewhere in my addled brain that this life of mine was not up to speed. I had a husband and we adored each other; I had two healthy, raucous sons; I had a job that paid enough and a career that, while not setting a blaze anywhere, gave me complete satisfaction. And still I found myself miserable, assured that I was lacking – what? . . . Something. . . . I was lacking something: the right high-heel shoes, the money to reupholster the couch, time to really sink into writing, the enormous flush of excitement that comes with the first breath of love, the faith – in God, or mankind, or simply oneself – that allows many to merely shrug off this sort of lassitude and get on with things.

What I decided I needed was a feast, and so I wheedled an invitation to one sponsored by the society from a woman I worked with. Laurie was a highly competent production editor at the magazine, but when she wasn't at the office she was with her fellow society members. She was a little younger than I was, small and pretty with long blond hair, and possessing a temperament as vicious as a rabid Chihuahua when some fool (particular members of the advertising staff) crossed her path. I was safe from her venom because my duties rarely involved her, but what drew us close together was my willingness to listen to her talk about the society. Laurie had two identities. Her interest in making mead required her to don a long skirt and a loose-fitting blouse cinched with a tightly laced bodice and to be known as something like Elespeth the brewer. Other times, with no special skills on display, she was a baroness, decked out in heavy embroidery and tapestry, the low square neck of her silk, velvet, or satin bodice edged with pearls or glass gems.

What really intrigued me was Laurie's sewing: she was one of the most gifted seamstresses I have ever encountered. She was in such demand that, if the rewards were sufficient, she would sometimes even cross borders and make a coronation robe or court gown for rival kingdoms. The garments she made were as masterful as those produced in a couture's atelier, created with fine French seams, hand-turned flat hems, and the nearly invisible stitching that assures a beautiful fit. Often Laurie's creations were embellished with designs done in glass beads and seed pearls; a detachable sleeve would be edged in handmade lace; a silk chemise delicately formed with hundreds of narrow tucks. Laurie worked diligently through the morning on whatever had to be done for the magazine, but by early afternoon her desk was cleared of film and print schedules to become crowded instead with bits and pieces of opulent fabric that she spent the rest of the day turning into a masterpiece.

Whenever I was bored or between projects, there wasn't anything more intriguing to me than to head down the corridor to see what Laurie was working on. While I watched her small hands deftly work a silver needle through thick upholstery and slippery silks, she told me stories about her kingdom's gatherings and the goings-on at the workshops the members held in things like smithing, bread making, sword fighting, and sidesaddle riding. I liked to hear about the back-stabbing and political maneuvering that occurred whenever a new king and queen were being coronated. And when Laurie returned from the Pennsylvania campsite where the society's Pennsic Wars were held each year, I was eager to see her photographs of makeshift tents, the long trestle tables laden with food, the men and women going about in polished armor and gaudy dress – the meandering charges across a heat-shimmering field ringed not with horses or wagons but with RVs and fancy four-wheel-drive vehicles.

I wish I could say I was simply amused by all of this, but that would not be the truth; the vision of another time and world – fanciful and playfully perfect – suited my strong desire to be anyone other than who I was. If I had thought about the reality of the Middle Ages – a period in which a woman over thirty was either long dead or considered more over-the-hill than she would be in our own society – I suppose I would have questioned my attraction, but as I said, I was as addled as a person can be in the throws of such a crisis, and I truly wanted to be a part of this romantic fabrication – among the tents and the spirited knights, sipping wine from a pewter goblet, waiting to be asked to dance (or even to learn) a *volta*.

"You should come to our Twelfth Night banquet," Laurie said out of the blue one day as I sat beside her desk, mesmerized by the glint of the needle piercing the soft surface of a blue velvet stomacher. I couldn't accept her invitation fast enough, but there was a problem: I had nothing to wear.

"All you need is a bodice, and I'll teach you how to make one. Then you can borrow one of my skirts."

What a treat! A bodice and a fancy banquet! And I had just the material for it – a piece of deep red silk I had purchased long ago, seduced by the color and the soft texture, but until that moment I was at a loss about what to do with it. I saw myself tightly laced into a red bodice, entranced by how the candlelight would make the color glow; what a sensation it would be to walk into a room wearing something as beautiful as I know it would be under Laurie's guidance, and how it would salvage – if only for a swift moment and if only before a few strangers – a woman who was feeling herself slide into oblivion. Upon hearing about the Twelfth Night invitation, my good-natured husband merely shook his head in bemusement. He liked the idea of the bodice, but the banquet was, for him, out of the question, especially if it meant he was required to pull on tights. That was fine; I would go myself.

All through the autumn, I worked on the bodice – a small article of clothing that proved to be as intricately constructed as the Golden Gate Bridge. A medieval bodice resembles a corset and consists of a front and back piece joined together by laces either on the sides or down the back (and sometimes both). Laurie constructed her bodices with whalebones and stiff linen interfacing, which allowed them to stand on their own like sculptures but also flattened and then thrust forward a woman's breasts in an outwardly appealing manner. Since metal rivets weren't invented until the early nineteenth century, each eyelet (as many as twenty on a side, depending on how long the bodice is) was hand sewn, using silk embroidery thread and the tiniest of stitches executed in a precise, overhanded looping manner.

We closed the door to Laurie's office to take my measurements, and then spread the red silk on the floor to cut the pattern. I am, at best, little more than a journeyman sewer, but I was determined now to make the finest bodice anyone had ever seen. Laurie showed me how to secure the linen interfacing between the silk so that it would stay flat and where to sew the pockets for the eight narrow whalebones. For accuracy, we looked at pictures of gowns historians had retrieved from the stone sepulchers of the dust-reduced nobility – only the front of the garments survived, while the back, subjected to the weight and disintegration of the body, became an X-ray-like image stained on the tomb's floor. Better preserved were those garments found when the Thames was dredged. Some had been discarded in the water or lost in the tide by careless laundresses; others were what remained after the fish had had their fill of the clothing's occupant, the river's cold and muddy depths proving to be a fine preserver for textiles. My bodice would actually be in the style favored by the upper middle class and nobility in the years just before the beginning of the Renaissance. It would not, however, be as ornate as many of them were; I did not want gems strewn across the front, no fine embroidery or slashes to allow a chemise to be pulled through in captivating little puffs. My bodice would be plain, with nothing to distract from the dazzling color or the daring neckline.

While we sewed, Laurie instructed me on the minutiae of medieval dining. The Twelfth Night celebration was to be held in the rectory of an old church that the society had rented for the occasion in a New Jersey suburb. The menu would be a variation of the one prepared for the marriage of the ten-year-old Alexander III of Scotland to the eleven-year-old Margaret, daughter of England's Henry III, that took place in York on December 26, 1251 – a feast that required, in part, 300 deer, 7,000 hens, 70 boars, 68,500 loaves of bread, and about 25,000 gallons of wine. The society's feast, of course, would be a mere shadow of that giant event. It would begin with *furmentry*, a soup of ground wheat and almonds, and then proceed to *blaundsorr* (a rice porridge), *glazed pilgrim* (some kind of fish deftly boiled at the head, fried in the middle, and roasted at the tail), a haunch of beef roasted on a spit in the rectory's fireplace, a *Spectacle* composed of a pie stuffed (after the crust was baked) with live toads that would amusingly come hopping out when the servants removed the top, a pair of geese stuffed with spices, and finally several different cakes, fruit, and a punch.

There would be three long tables arranged in a U shape in the middle of the rectory hall, providing enough room for the forty members who were expected to attend. On a platform behind the middle table would be a smaller table with a canopy fixed above it where the king and queen would sit. The rest of the gathering would take their places by rank at the lower tables, with the king's favorite courtiers immediately before the royal couple and, on either side of them, those of lesser station – bishops, mitered abbots, marquesses, earls, and barons, then knights, mayors, and town officials. Way at the end – or even at a table of their own in the corner – would be servants, townsfolk, and hangers-on. Laurie advised me to find a suitable drinking cup; she had a silver goblet, but glass, so long as it was thick and hand blown, would do. There would be knives but no forks or spoons; nearly everyone except peasants brought their own cloth napkins.

And which, I asked, of her personas – the brewing wench or the fine lady – would she be attending as, I asked, since it would decide where we sat.

"I'll have to see at the next meeting what they need more of," she hastily replied, and it worried me to think I might end up groveling at the servant table in my lovely red bodice.

I like to think it was perhaps this bit of shameful classism that nudged me into examining why I was, in fact, going to this dinner. Toads and stuffed goose and all those rules about who sat where! What was I doing with all of this? But still I worked on the bodice, and when all that was left to do was to make the eyelids, I gave it to Laurie, who I knew would do a better job than I ever could. It was two weeks before Christmas when she brought it back to me. I ran my hands longingly across its cool, perfect surface and would have slipped it on right there except for the many pairs of eyelets I had to lace the ribbons through, not to mention the work piled precariously on my desk. I left early though, and on the subway ride home I threaded the ribbons through the small holes, imaging how I would ignore the kids and the evening's chores to run into my bedroom and try the bodice on. But then I opened the front door and, as always, was consumed by the night's routine of hugs and homework and listening to a spouse's day; cooking and eating and leaving the dishes for more hugs and dog walks and screams and a fight between brothers, followed by stories and more stories and tucks and hugs and, at last, collapse. It wasn't until the children were asleep and my husband was lost in a book that I could retreat to the bedroom, remove my top, and finally squeeze into the bodice, pulling the ribbons tight, feeling the fabric's chill and the unbending spokes of bone pressing my breasts even flatter than they were, causing both an enticing and annoying discomfort.

"What is that?" Chris exclaimed as he suddenly came behind me.

"A medieval bodice," I replied in a squeezed and measured voice.

His hand reached tentatively out toward my bound waist. "This is what you're wearing to that banquet thing?"

I looked at myself in the mirror wearing this beautiful and ridiculous bodice. No, I thought to answer him, my desire to loiter in the past fading. His hands slid slowly up the sides, his fingers weaving between the laces. I forgot to pine for the exhilarating flair of first love and felt instead the fervor of a long intimacy: enough time and money and the right high heels – all these things fell into their proper place as my husband unknotted the laces and loosened the constricting bodice. In place of all these foolish wants and shallow desires came faith – the kind that builds on the past, on pilings constructed from both disasters and triumphs – that I would move from this muddled age into a fruitful renaissance.

And so, there was no *Spectacle* of toad pie for me, no ***blaundsorr*** or *furmentry* either. Laurie was more than disappointed, but she did not yap at me. For the few more months I stayed at that job, I continued to visit her in her office and marvel over her sewing, but her gowns and stories no longer held as strong an attraction for me.

When Twelfth Night came that year, I made my own feast of warming pumpkin soup, a roasted goose stuffed with fruit, almonds, and spices and, for dessert, a *Spectacle*, a plum tart that had perched at its center a small toy bird I stole from my eldest son's Christmas stocking. All through the night, I poured my guests a rich red wine and let them sit wherever they pleased, and, under a velvet shirt, I wore my red bodice – with the bones removed and not as tightly laced.

Death Was Meant for This

There is no end to their trickery.

MARTIN LUTHER, ON MERCHANTS

Several accounts describe how the plague first reached Europe in the mid-fourteenth century, and most of them involve spice merchants. The simplest one entails a single ship, more populated with rats than men. By the time the ship docked, the flea-lousy rodents scurried happily off the boat while the men were either carried away to their unsuspecting families or, for expediency's sake, their bodies were thrown overboard, contaminating the local water. My favorite theory, however, which illustrates much about this time between the close of one age and the beginning of another, involves a small intrepid band of Italian merchants on a scouting and looting expedition through the spice-rich Near East who so enraged the locals in the Crimea with their high-handed business practices that they were forced to seek refuge within the walls of the citadel at Kaffa. When none of their weapons succeeded in evicting the merchants, the citizens took to catapulting plague victims – already dead or nearly so – over the walls and into the citadel compound before retreating. The merchants, puzzled by the sudden cessation of hostilities but relieved to be left alone, sneaked back to their ships and set sail for home, unaware that their souls would arrive in heaven long before their bodies reached familiar shores.

From Italy, the Black Death skipped into France at the port of Marseilles, then sailed on up to London, effectively putting a stop to all the gaiety and pageantry of the High Middle Ages wherever it landed. From 1347 to 1353 death seemed to be a guest in every small village and great city and at all the banquets, liturgies, and royal courts. Exact tallies are hard to come by, but the number of victims succumbing to the disease can be reckoned by the villages devoid of life almost overnight, the deserted cloisters left to fall into ruin, the cultivated fields that returned to wilderness, the nobles and royalty suddenly bereft of heirs and serfs, the orphans fending for themselves in a lifeless world. The Black Death did not discriminate: it took the poor, the wealthy, the sainted, and the sinner. Doctors, dying themselves in great numbers, searched through their meager textbooks and turned to the Arab world for a cure. They came up with many, including more than a few in which saffron was seen as a great benefit. As in Roman times, people were advised to purify the air in their homes by sprinkling saffron on the floor or burning it in the hearth – a recommendation that only the rich could afford to practice in sufficient quantity to harvest any benefit. One popular prescription was this, recorded by Elizabeth, Countess of Kent:

An Excellent Receipt for the Plague

Take 1 pound green walnuts, ½ ounce of saffron, ½ ounce London Treacle. Beat them together in a mortar and with a little cordial or some such water. Vapour it over the fire until it becomes electuary (syrupy). Keep this in a pot and take as much as a walnut (probably referring to dose size) and it is good to cure the plague.

(If you want to try this recipe out, it probably won't kill you, but it won't cure the plague either.)

The gleeful effect of all this desolation was to sweep away a great deal of feudalism's injustice and inequalities. The sheer scarcity of common country and city workers made those who were left such a rare commodity that they were invested with new bargaining power. The nobility gradually found themselves having to make concessions to their serfs, and if their great estates were not to be left to rot, a more favorable system of landownership would have to be established. The powers of the Holy Church – so impotent against the strength of the plague – came into doubt, rendering suspect the substantial wealth and political influence of its many well-kept princes. Artisans and tradespeople united into guilds in order to take more control of what they could charge for their labor and as a result found themselves rising into a social class that had not been allowed on earth since ancient times – the solid middle class with resources and means that almost put them beyond the tired authority of the old nobility.

It was a slippery, tumultuous time to navigate – the words *avaricious* and *cruel* are often used to describe these years in which everyone seems to be grasping to get a little for their own, to take a sip of that old simple brew of power and money. It is in such a climate that one of history's most curious ruckuses transpired. It happened in 1374, between Austria and the small independent city of Basle, an important hub for trade that enjoyed considerable prosperity. For Austria, however, the preceding years had been especially difficult. Before the plague even hit, the country had suffered through years of bad harvests, drought, and an earthquake that left many of its citizens convinced the second coming was near; then the plague swept through, slaying, by one estimate, a quarter of the country's population. The kingdom was almost impoverished, and so the nobles, in order to improve their lot, began to claim the rich land on either side of the Rhine as their own. In a bow to the changing times and in acknowledgment of their weakening authority, the nobles also took to demanding seats on the local town councils so that if any one should dare contest their claim, they could – within the letter of the law – vote them down. Towns up and down the Rhine complained that the noble members of their councils rarely showed up for meetings unless there was something of interest to them on the agenda and generally acted as if the newly prosperous citizens and urban centers stilled owed them some sort of continuing patronage.

Yet despite such grumbling, the nobles were allowed to take their seats – and the land – until they came to the city of Basle, which felt itself to be in a better position to resist. The town mustered up a unit of guerrilla fighters who went out into the surrounding forest and began to harass the nobles, sometimes by scaring away the prey and disrupting their hunting parties, other times by actually taking up sniper positions in the trees and ravines to fire on them. The situation went on like this for a few months until the nobles got their fill of such insolence and decided to strike back in kind. A group of them intercepted "a great train of merchandise, containing eight hundred pounds of saffron," and hijacked it to a neighboring castle.

There was nothing accidental about what the nobles chose to abduct. For a trade city to lose any goods would be distressing, but to lose such costly goods would surely have been devastating. After the advent of the plague, the price of saffron had only risen. Demand for it had increased across the population because it had proved to be so valuable as a medicine, and yet, at the same time, there were now fewer people in Europe to grow and harvest it. Merchants were forced to import it from other countries, often by making a steep investment from their own funds to procure it. They did so knowing that, in such an economy, saffron commanded an enormous price and would allow them to recoup their money many times over. Moreover, because of lingering hostilities from the Crusades in much of the Moslem and Arab world, the best-quality saffron that could extract top dollar was hard to come by, if not be completely unavailable. The Basle shipment was recorded as coming from Rhodes, still as excellent a source as it had once been considered in Rome, and which was at the time under the able rule of Venice. The wholesale market value for such a stock (comparable shipments are recorded to have been worth, in U.S. equivalency, at least five hundred thousand dollars) would have represented a sizable asset to Basle's financial status.

The Saffron War was on! It lasted fourteen weeks and was not resolved until Leopold of Austria arbitrated a deal with the bishop of Basle. The saffron was returned to the town, but the bishop was forced to pay the nobles for their expenses during the course of the war and give up the nearby town of Kleinbasel to Leopold. The bishop did just that, and hostilities ceased, but Basle's merchants were shaken by the ordeal. They felt they could no longer risk their fortunes on any more saffron shipments from Italy.

In any case, the trade routes were densely populated with thieves on the lookout for caravans, and although the great merchant ships of both Venice and Genoa were routinely escorted by these cities' powerful navies, whole cargoes were often lost to pirates. And given a choice between saffron and almost anything else – including gold – pirates and highway robbers alike would ignore the gold and take the saffron because it was less trouble to transport and worth about the same – if not more. In such unsure conditions, the citizens of Basle saw an opportunity and began to plant their own crop. By 1420, the council proclaimed, "a course of events has arisen which should be a profitable venture for the merchants of Basle, namely the fact that many people, nobles and common, have now begun to grow saffron which appears to be coming on well." The municipality adopted the flower in their coat of arms and grew exceedingly wealthy. Other cities, seeing Basle's success, begged for corms, "for they envied the Basle merchant-growers, the city council, and even the dean and chapter of Basle cathedral, who received tithes of every fruit borne of the earth." But strict laws were enacted, and it was forbidden to sell the corms to anyone outside the city walls. Bailiffs were posted in the fields to patrol against those who would steal the flowers or dig up the corms; if any were caught, they were promptly banished from the region forever.

Saffron grew well in Basle for ten years, and then it mysteriously began to wither. The flowers pushed up small, only to open upon puny threads; the corms turned soft in the ground. Perhaps the citizens were too concerned with monetary output and worked the fields too hard. Or perhaps a blight – not uncommon to old flower bulbs – worked its way beneath the ground. To an experienced gardener, such sudden failures are not surprising. But what is surprising to anyone with even the briefest relationship to saffron is how little it was truly regarded in the town. For through that long decade – and even before when so much of it was sold in its market, Basle did not see saffron as anything but a valuable commodity. No fond recipes of saffron dishes were written down; no one seemed to consider taking a sip of a saffron-infused wine; not even the violent scent of the drying threads – soporific and permeating as it is – left behind any impression. After a few years of little return for their labor, Basle abandoned its tired fields and began once more to import whatever saffron their customers needed. Yet it is hard indeed not to consider that saffron – abused and underappreciated – decided to quit Basle first.

By the middle of the fifteenth century, Nuremberg had become the main marketplace for goods coming into central Europe from the

Mediterranean. Situated at the crossroads of the major trade routes and surrounded by an excellent network of rivers and well-built bridges for easy transportation, the city took its position seriously and enacted laws to bring some semblance of order and integrity to what was essentially, at most other marketplaces, a free-for-all. One of the first laws Nuremberg passed was the Safranschou, in 1358, to govern the inspection and quality of saffron. On any given day, there were at least seven different varieties of imported saffron for sale in the city's market – French, Spanish, Sicilian, Cretan, Austrian, Greek, and Turkish – all with their own subtle differences in taste and potency. In the late fall these were often joined by independent local growers who came to market hoping to better their situation for the winter with a small harvest from their garden patch.

The large sacks of imported saffron and the small bowls of locally grown threads were grouped together in Nuremberg's large and bustling central market. So much saffron mingled together, the dark red threads seemingly indistinguishable from one another. A wily merchant may have stood by his sack and looked at his neighbor's, or perhaps a poor farmer stole a glance at another's pile, and both may have thought about what they could do with the extra profit if only they had just a little more saffron to sell. Just a little more, or a little heavier – both made possible, perhaps, with a handful of red marigold petals crumbled among the threads, or even lily stymies mixed in at the bottom. Some also soaked their threads in honey before they were dried and thus increased their weight. Martin Luther wrote to the Christian nobles that he had even heard of "the trick of placing such spices as pepper, ginger and saffron in damp vaults to increase their weight." Still, the avaricious merchant and the hungry farmer would both make peace with their Maker by claiming it was only a small bit of trickery and of no great harm to anyone. Wasn't one speck of saffron potent enough to color a whole yard of silk or sooth an old man's stomach? What would a few marigold petals do but mellow the brew?

The Nuremberg judges saw things differently, and those who broke the Safranschou law by adulterating saffron were thrown into the Loch – the hole at the bottom of the dungeon in the Nuremberg jail. The hole measured two square yards and two yards high, a dark, cold hollow carved from the bedrock the prison was built on. Lying on the brackish floor, a prisoner's ear would quickly fill with fellow prisoners' moans and ravings that echoed in whispered waves through the stones. Sometimes, in a brief moment of quiet before dawn, the river that lapped at the base of the prison could be heard and smelled – its fresh scent turned instantly putrid within that brutish place.

Confession was wise for the soul – a clean break of the crime before punishment was metered out – but if none came, then the offending merchant or poor farmer was taken from the hole and led through a doorway above which were carved the Latin words

Ad mala patrata haec sunt atra theatra parata.
(For perpetrated evils are these dark theaters prepared.)

to find themselves in a chamber full of racks and chains and burning embers.

It should be remembered that these were lawless times; rulers had lost their ability to cow their subjects with mere commands. Kingdoms were falling apart, borders were crumbling, unruly frontiers were everywhere; in such a world law and order were imposed by punishment, harsh and swift. Murders, turncoats, and heretics all received the death penalty, but so did those who damaged property at night or who failed at suicide attempts. Some were executed for eating meat on Friday; a servant could be hung for letting his eyes linger a little too long on his master's wife. And those who sought to make an extra profit by changing the weight of their merchandise or adulterating their food products forfeited their life.

In swift measure, all the guilty were taken outside to the crowd that gathered on the prison's bridge. On busy days, they were just hung – Christians near the prison walls, Jews further out on the gallows suspended above the river. If there was time and their crime high, many were drawn and quartered. Hans Kolbele, a merchant who must have tremendously annoyed the judges, was first dragged behind a horse until all his bones were shattered, then stretched across a stone slab and eviscerated and finally stuffed into his grave, his lips gasping for breath the way a hooked fish will do at the bottom of a boat. Bags of his impure saffron were packed into his mouth, and then he was sealed into his grave.

Jobst Finderlers was spared the drawing and quartering and merely burned, his saffron used as part of the kindling, which probably anointed the city's air with a powerful scent that lingered for days. Elss Pfnognerin was not drawn and quartered either, but that was more for modesty's sake since it was considered indelicate for an executioner to expose a woman's belly and muck around in her bowels. Instead, at least in Nuremberg until 1515, when the executioner requested to drown them, women were buried alive. Adulterers were buried with their lovers; one poor woman who was found to have killed her baby after a hard labor was sealed with the infant under a large stone slab in a field just outside the city's limits. Elss was said to have lost her husband to syphilis (known as the French disease) a few years before, and without any help, their farm had fallen to ruin. She kept a neat garden, and her house was clean, but the small pouch of saffron she brought to market that November was not. The ground would have already been frozen – or partially so. In any case, it would have been hard against her back, chilling her bones when the executioner laid her down in the hollow he had prepared for her. Was there a priest to murmur some prayers for her? Did anyone in the crowd protest that for such a deed – a small understandable deed – this was all too much? If they did, it did not matter. Elss's small heap of saffron that she had pinned so much hope on was sprinkled across her body, and then she was sealed into the ground, her screams and tears and pleas growing fainter with each layer of stone and dirt. It is said that in due course an uncle came for her four small children and took them away from Nuremberg to live with him in the country.

The one consolation in contemplating someone being smothered with saffron is the old Persian belief that it took away melancholy, and perhaps – just perhaps – these victims of a cruel justice were made delirious, their pain lessened by the very stuff that had condemned them. I do not know. But I think that I have felt saffron's anesthetizing qualities dull a pain so sharp and deep that months later I can still feel its presence.

That experience came just a few moments after my mother died. My sister and brother and I had stood at her bedside for most of the night and through the morning until, at noon, with a few shivers and a sigh, our mother passed. There was nothing more for us to do. We had held her hand, stroked her forehead, bathed her body to take away the last of her fever. My sister, Sue, who in her profession tends to many dying people, did what she could to take away the pain and give her peace; my brother, Joe, in all his strength, had held her tightly. When she finally left us alone, we stepped back from her bed, and as we turned to depart each of us out of long habit, I suppose, called out goodbye – "See you," we said – and were halfway down the hall before we fully realized what we had done.

We were tired and drawn, dazed – and famished. Of all the things that go through your mind when you watch death approach, thinking of food may seem the most absurd, maybe even a little obscene. And yet it is what the living almost always turn to, feeling a need not only to fill an emptiness but also to almost deny the presence of death. A sort of feasting occurs that is in no way affirmative but rather simply and quite insistently the living's way of breaking away, the body understanding before the mind fully does what is the necessary and correct order demanded in the wider world. I know my sister and I had not really eaten in days; it was probably the same with my brother, and so through the last hours of our vigil I had sat composing a dinner to make that night – something with red meat, thick with flavors – something that would demand a bottle of good wine and a rich dessert.

"Crème brûlée," Sue demanded as we stood outside trying to get our minds around what to do next.

"I'll bring the wine," Joe added. And then we went off to the church and the cemetery and the funeral home, the thought of the evening dinner keeping us together through the long day. We were in no shape to go grocery shopping after we were finished doing what we had to do, but somehow Sue and I pushed the cart up and down the busy aisles, going along in a sort of mindless stupor among the usual Saturday throng, our eyes catching on the warm yellow of new tulips, on the ruby sheen of red onions. We searched for something thick and filling. Pinwheels of beef stuffed with dried tomatoes and prosciutto was what we finally settled on, as well as small white potatoes, a simple salad, black olives, and a soft cheese.

After we got home and unpacked the groceries, we told each other we would take a nap. Sue went off to her room, but I couldn't sit still, let alone lie down, falling into the restlessness I remembered from the last time I had lost a parent. So I made a cup of strong tea and set about making the crème brûlée that somehow turned into a pie. Anyone who knows me understands that I would rather make a pie than almost anything else, and that is one reason crème brûlée became a pie, but the real thing I was after was to lose myself through this endless afternoon in the involved work of making a crust. But I couldn't find my sister's flour and instead came upon some stale *biscotti*. I made a crumb crust, baked it for five minutes until it had just formed a crust, then let it cool while I made the custard. In an attempt to hold at bay the first strong touches of melancholy, I did as Alexander himself might have done and added to the hot cream a fine dose of saffron from the bottle Sue brought back from our travels in Spain (which I will tell you about later). A quantity slightly bigger than a generous pinch, the threads filled the hollow in my cupped palm, and I crushed them a little between my fingers before I threw them into the pot of cream. I beat the yolks and whisked in the hot cream, saffron's perfume rising in the air with each beat of the whisk.

Sue got up from her nap just as I was putting the pie in the oven. Joe and his family arrived a half hour later as I pulled it from the oven. His children spread out through the house, while the adults – Sue and Joe and I, along with Joe's fine wife – settled around the table, pouring wine and nibbling on the olives and cheese. Relatives and my husband and sons, Sue's daughters, and the last of our parents' friends would all begin to crowd around us in the following days, but for now there were just the three of us – all that remained of our family – and as the long day finally came to an end, we drew close together, the sorrow loosening for a moment while we sank, talking and laughing, with comfort and longing into this hard-won meal.

Saffron Crème Brûlée Pie

This recipe was influenced by a crème brûlée I tasted in Consuegra, a village in Spain where a saffron festival is held each year (see the chapter

"Fiesta de la Rosa del Azafran"). The crème brûlée was the last dish I had at the restaurant, and I can still taste the chilled cream beneath the warm brittle topping. The saffron flavor was not pronounced, but it was there, causing the custard to turn golden and adding a mysterious sharp slap to its flavor.

For the crust:

2 cups cookie crumbs
(any kind – vanilla or chocolate wafers; biscotti work very well)
6 tablespoons (¾ stick) sweet butter, melted

Preheat oven to 400 degrees. If the cookies are whole, put them in the bowl of a food processor fitted with a metal blade and pulse until the cookies have become fine crumbs. Mix the melted butter into the crumbs until they just begin to come together. Pour into a deep 9-inch pie plate and press into the sides and on the bottom, more thickly on the bottom than on the sides.

Bake in the oven for five minutes until the crust just begins to brown and firm. Remove and let cool while you make the filling.

For the filling:

2⅓ cups heavy cream
⅔ cup milk
¼ cup granulated sugar
¼ to ½ teaspoon saffron – depending on taste (begin with the smallest amount to see if you like it)
3 whole eggs
3 egg yolks
1 teaspoon vanilla extract
¾ cup brown sugar

Preheat oven to 300 degrees. Stir the cream, milk, and sugar together in a medium-sized saucepan. Heat over a medium burner, and when it begins to get warm add the saffron. Bring almost to a boil and then remove from the heat.

In a separate bowl, beat the eggs, extra yolks, and vanilla extract together until they are thick. Gradually add the hot cream to the egg mixture, whisking the whole time. When all the cream has been added, return the mixture to the saucepan and cook over moderate heat, stirring constantly with a wooden spoon, until the custard coats the back of the spoon. Remove from heat and pour into the crumb crust.

Set the pie plate in a large pan and place in the middle of the oven. Pour enough hot water into the outer pan to come at least three-quarters of the way up the pie plate. Bake for 35 minutes until the center of the custard is set. When done, remove and let cool; chill until ready to serve.

Right before serving, preheat broiler. Sift brown sugar across the top of the custard and set the pie under the broiler as close to the heating element as possible. Broil until the sugar is a rich brown but not burned. Observe carefully. Remove at once and serve.

I know people – myself included – who think nothing of lying on the kitchen floor, no matter what they're wearing or how elegant the occasion (or what state their floor is in) to make sure the sugar forms a nice crust. It's the only way to guarantee you'll get the best result, but it's also sort of nice lying there in that awkward position, filled with anticipation and apprehension, as the flames warm your face and dance across the melting sugar.

The Making of a Town

It maketh the English sprightly.

FRANCIS BACON, ON SAFFRON, QUOTED IN

History of Cultivated Vegetables by Henry Phillips, 1623

It is a small mystery how saffron arrived in the English town of Walden and worked such influence that the town became known as Saffron Walden. The weakest hunch centers around Sir Thomas Smith, a secretary of state under the great Elizabeth, who in 1513 was born in Walden. For this fact to be of any merit to our tale, Sir Thomas would have to have been born with a spade and several corms clutched in his wee fists, since saffron was already a fairly important cash crop by the time he first saw the light of day. A more probable story opens around 1350, during the reign of Edward III, with saffron taking quite well to England's eastern coast. The stars of this story are sometimes the Knights of St. John of Jerusalem, who are said to have plundered bushels of corms and brought them home from northern Palestine after the loss of Acre in the last Crusade. However, the trouble with this version is that the knights were known to have sown their corms only on farms belonging to their order, and these were in the north country. On top of that, they were a tight-fisted bunch and kept their saffron supply to themselves.

In his *Principal Navigations, Voyages, Traffics, and Discoveries of the English Nation* (1598) Richard Hakluyt promotes a more egalitarian character:

> *It is reported at Saffron Walden that a Pilgrim, purposing to do good to his countrey, stole an head of Saffron and hid the same in his Pilgrim's staffe, which he had made hollow before of purpose, and so he brought this root into the realme with venture of his life; for, if he had bene taken, by the law of the countrey from whence it came, he had died for the fact.*

A brave and plucky English lad would certainly have warmed the hearts of Hakluyt's readers, but many now consider him a rather shameless storyteller.

Reason would lead to a much more base and boring saga: with the Saffron War waging in Basle and greedy pirates trolling the seas, an enterprising farmer or two would surely have latched on to the idea that a killing could be gained from the spice-daffy rich and noble with a homegrown crop of saffron. If Swiss farmers could muster up a steady supply, why not the English from their blessedly fruitful countryside? As for how the corms traveled from their sunny native lands to the dank British isle in the first place, it is more than likely they made the voyage centuries before in the pockets of homesick Roman soldiers, though it probably took the Crusades – or pilgrims coming home from their travels – to remind the natives that the pretty autumn flower blooming in their midst was actually worth something. (And once the Crusades made it safe – as well as fashionable – to travel to the Holy Lands, pilgrims did hurry home with a wealth of exotic souvenirs hidden in hollowed-out walking sticks and tied beneath the conveniently heavy folds of skirts and veils.) Then our industrious farmers would only have had to dig up the corms that had naturalized, and after some years of careful cultivation, they would have realized the beginnings of a thriving saffron trade.

At one time or another, saffron was planted all around England, particularly in Norfolk and Suffolk, but nowhere did it last so long, nor bloom as prolifically, as it did in the eastern coastal province of Essex. This part of England had once been submerged under a primordial sea whose ancient floor was thick with the oozy skeletal remains of tiny *Protozoic foraminiferas;* when the tide retreated, the calcium-rich ooze remained, drying and hardening to form chalk that lightened the soil and improved its drainage. Buried in such a delightful medium, the corms were kept almost as dry as they would have been on shimmering Crete, as content to flourish in abundant radiance as they did on the sunbaked Persian plains.

But, frankly, that saffron blossomed so comfortably outside its native lands is not such a noteworthy occurrence. After all, it had settled in Switzerland quite nicely and for many years gave no outward signs of missing either broiling heat or the near-drought conditions of the Mediterranean and the Middle East. Yet the Swiss crop did eventually fail, whereas the English crop – with the exception of a couple of ill-timed autumn rains – never truly did. And that is indeed a remarkable feat that can be attributed only to a certain madness that is known to affect the British population. The English have many attributes, but chief among them has to be their inclination to garden (of which farming should be seen as only a larger manifestation of their particular mania to grow things). They don't stop at just growing plants, either. They collect and draw and at seemingly inexhaustible length ponder a plant's habits, residence, character, and manner, as if what they really wish to do is to crawl right inside even the most delicate stem in expectation of finding the elusive truths of earthly life nestled sweetly at its core.

When one looks closely at the matter, it seems that nearly every person capable of writing in the fifteenth and sixteenth centuries took quill to paper and recorded their considerable opinion of just how and when saffron should be grown. There is, to start, Gilbert of Hayland's proclamation that "saffron is related to wisdom," followed by John Gerard, in his famous *Herbal,* who declares with great authority how the corms "doth first rise out of the ground nakedly in September, and his long small grassie leaves shortly after, never bearing floure and leafe at once."

The Rev. William Harrison, the rector of the parish five miles down the road from Walden, made this contribution to the 1587 edition of *Holinshed's Chronicles,* a long description of how the neighboring saffron farmers, who were known as Crokers, cultivated their fields:

> *The heads of saffron are raised [turned out of the ground] in July, either wyth plough or spade; and being scowred from theyr Rose and severed from such heades as are ingendered of them since the last setting, they are enterred againe out of hand by rankes or rowes; and, being covered wyth moulds, they rest in the earth, where they cast forth little filets and small rotes like unto a scalion, untill September; in the beginning of whych moneth, ye ground is pared and all weedes and grasses that groweth upon the same removed, to the intente that nothing may annoy the flower when his time doth come to rise . . . in the later ende of the aforesayd moneth, the flower beginneth to appeare. . . . These flowers are gathered in the mornyng, before the rising of the Sunne, whych would cauce them to welke; and the chives are picked from the flowers, these latter are throwne into the dung hill, the [chives] being dryed upon little kelles [kilns] covered wyth straigned canvasses over a soft fire; whereby, and by the waight that is layed upon them, they are dried and pressed into cakes, and then bagged up for ye benefite of theyr owners.*

And this is but one (although the most dominant) of the many tracts printed at the time to argue the fine differences in planting techniques, of which the most agreed upon appears to have been to sow the corms three inches apart in rows that were themselves three inches apart. Points of contention swirled instead around how long a field should rest between sowing – with some advocating seven years and others voting for five. Harrison, who seems to have been the most carefully observant of men, stated in a later edition of the *Chronicles* that it should be twenty years between plantings to assure the most potent crop. All acknowledged, however, that a field should not be in production for more than three years. It should then be turned under and rejuvenated with a crop of barley. The Honorable Charles Howard (no less a personage than the eldest son of the Earl of Suffolk, master of Audley End, and an original Fellow of the Royal Society!) weighed in on the matter in *his* saffron account by siding with the seven-year crowd, for that seemed in his experience to be enough time to assure that an acre would "yield, at least, twelve pounds of good Saffron. . . . and in some years twenty pounds."

Howard goes on to give a very detailed computing of the expenses involved in producing saffron, but in his reckoning the expense and considerable labor is offset by the guaranteed princely profit of some twenty pounds sterling per annum.

Such was England's success that there seems to have been only one major crop failure – and that was blamed not on technique but on divine retaliation. The trouble began in 1556; for two hundred years autumn had brought a purple blush to Walden's fields, and this year was no exception. In fact, the yield had been so great that in the Reverend Harrison's account, "Some of the townes men of Walden gave one half of the floures for picking of the other, and sent them ten to twelve miles aboard into the countries."

But other farmers were not inclined to share their wealth; on the contrary, they wished to restrict further saffron production to keep the prices (and their own profits) up. Instead of being thankful for their abundant crop, these farmers went about Walden murmuring,

> *in a most blasphemous manner [that] "God did now shite Saffron"; . . . so the Lord, considering theyr unthankfullnesses, gave them ever since such scarcities as the greatest murmurers have now the least store, and moste of them are eyther worne out of occyupying or remain scarce able to maintain their grounds wythout the helpe of other men.*

It is not recorded in what form God expressed his wrath – whether it was untimely rain or frost or the ground turning sour – but it took Walden close to twenty years to recuperate from this disgraceful episode. By 1586, the town was again being described as standing "in the midst of fields smiling with the most beautiful crocus," and in written accounts was generally referred to with full patriotic pride and glory as Saffron Walden.

In October, as the harvest was brought into town and the chives were torn from the flower, great heaps of rumpled petals drifted like purple snow across doorsteps and alleys and clogged the gutters of Walden's streets. The chives were dried in kilns and packed in leather pouches in time to be sold at the St. Ursula Fair held each year on the saint's feast day on October 21 in the center of town. (Of the many legends concerning Ursula and her martyrdom, most agree that she was a fourth-century Christian British princess – which would account for her feast day being so roundly celebrated – and that she was killed because she would not marry a pagan prince. Vast disagreements center on how many of her handmaidens shared her fate and where the slaughter took place, either Cologne or [in an English bid to be the discoverers of North America] the Virgin Islands.)

People came to the fair from all over – including merchants from the Continent – to stock their winter supplies. The boom age for English saffron was from the sixteenth through the early eighteenth century, years when it was considered to be the best in the world and easily commanded the highest price – sometimes as high as twice as much as the varieties brought with great difficulties from the Near East. The Essex farmers grew very rich indeed and honored the source of their wealth by chiseling into the face of public halls and bridges delicate renditions of the saffron flower in its brief moment of morning glory, open-faced or grouped in three blossoms, its slender threads etched as thick as veins.

And so it is surprising that saffron did not find a more abiding place in the society of its adopted country, for its use dwindled with the last embers of the Renaissance. It cannot even be said that it found a solid place as a dye – a shocking thought if you consider the fine reputation English weavers and their cloth enjoyed. In truth, they never seemed to bother themselves much with the dyeing end of cloth production, and when they did, they were considered by even their most ardent champions to be horrendous at the art. But what did it matter, really, when the superb dye vats of Flanders were just a short boat ride away? The English merely packed their best bolts of white cloth into their barges, shipped them off across the channel and, in a few weeks' time, their cloth returned, without fuss or stench, transformed into kaleidoscopic jewels. Most of what was dyed on English soil was stuff of the poorest – and weakest – sort, fit only for the rough fabric that was made or purchased by peasants, and certainly not worth the expenditure of the finest saffron threads. (One story has it that saffron-dyed cloth was banned in Ireland by Henry VIII because the Irish considered saffron such a powerful cleansing agent that they felt they didn't need to bathe if they wore shirts and dresses made from the cloth. England's natives at the time could not have smelled any sweeter than the Irish – saffron shirts or not – so Henry's chief concern might have been more to prevent an outbreak of disease and ensure the comfort of his occupying nobles.)

As for its use in cooking – saffron ebbed faster from the English kitchen than any other of the spices that had once graced the table. In general, as the medieval age gave way to the escalating wonders of exploration, dining – and therefore cooking – became plainer. Many of the spices once used with abandon were set aside or supplanted by new discoveries (such as capers, sugar cane, and vanilla) from expeditions to the Far East and the Americas. And the great quantities and elaborate preparations once deemed necessary for even the most common repast were reduced to a mere handful. The forty dishes that Henry IV demanded for his evening supper were reduced to ten for William and Mary. The growing appeal of puritanical severity made colorful dishes seem garish – almost wicked. Such was the repressive tenor of the time that even those who were inclined by nature toward luxury or could afford a bit of showing off found it more expedient to rein in their desires. And so you find the likes of Samuel Pepys tucking in contentedly (or so he insisted) to a pot of pease porridge with his wife for the evening meal, and Lord Sandwich eating but a joint of mutton all by himself in his great hall.

This new austerity can be ascribed in part to the continuing harassment of the plague. It again hit London hard in 1665 and spread from England back across the Continent, where it was thought to have at last seen its day. With fewer farmers and hunters to supply the table with food, especially meat, much of the population (though particularly in England) made do with bread and cheese washed down with brimming cups of good yeasty ale. Two pounds of bread and one pound of cheese was the daily allotment for soldiers in the field; across the countryside it was often far less. The Crown tried to encourage the fish trade – both to feed its subjects and to use its fleet of fishing boats as training grounds for sailors and shipbuilders – but supper, as well as breakfast and whatever could be scrounged together in the evening, was more than likely to consist mainly of bread.

It was in baking, then, that saffron found a more devoted home – enlivening fine cakes and breads often reserved for festive occasions and saints' days, whose recipes remain today very similar to what they were five hundred years ago. Curiously enough, none of these recipes can be proved to have originated in Essex or can even be said with firm authority to have been baked at anytime, anywhere, near Walden's saffron fields.

You must instead travel sheer across the island to Cornwall for the most famous recipe calling for saffron, and once you get there you will hear the neighborhood legend that saffron was introduced to these rocky shores not by anyone from Walden but rather by the intrepid, forever roving Phoenicians. If this is true (and there is no sensible reason for it not to be), the people of Cornwall would certainly have had to be content with at least a thousand years of fitful harvests in their damp, crocus-unfriendly climate, or they would have had to put up with the hazards of constant war and fierce seas to import it from Spain before they enjoyed a reliable supply from England's eastern coast.

The following version of the region's specialty comes from a collection of old recipes gathered from the readers of the *Daily Express* newspaper. The collection was published in 1971, but the contributor of this particular recipe, a Mrs. Lena Thomas from Marazion, Cornwall, relates that her mother wrote it down in 1911.

Cornish Saffron Cake

Set 2 ounces of yeast (1 package will do) to rise with a little sugar (½ teaspoon) and 1 tablespoon flour in a warm place. Soak about 5p worth of saffron – it used to be 3d worth 60 years ago! [use a good pinch, about 40 threads] – in a little boiling water. Mix 3 pounds flour and a pinch of salt with 1 lb lard [yes, lard], 4 ounces butter and 8 ounces sugar. Add 1 pound currants, 4 ounces sultanas, 4 ounces peels (lemon or orange). Add the yeast sponge and make a soft dough. Set this to rise for 3 hours. Knead into round "loaves" and place in warmed cake tins. Set to rise for 20 minutes longer. Bake in a moderate oven [350 degrees, preheated] for 1 hour.

[Depending on the size of the loaves you form, this will make 2 good-size loaves – or 4 smaller ones, which I can tell you from experience make very appreciated gifts. To make saffron buns, divide the dough into balls no bigger than your palm (you'll probably get at least a dozen from the dough), pat them into a bun shape and place them on a flat baking sheet. Allow the dough to rise for about 25 minutes, then bake at 375 degrees for about 12 to 15 minutes.]

In her lovely book *The Art of Cookery Made Plain and Easy* (1708), Hannah Glasse recorded the following recipe for another sort of saffron cake. I am transcribing it here in its original form – with modern measurement conversions given where useful in brackets – to give a good example of Mrs. Glasse's clear and pure language, which is one of the reasons why food historians love her so, but it is simply a source of quaint pleasure to the rest of us mortals.

To Make a Fine Seed or Saffron Cake

You must take a quarter of a peck of fine flour [about 4 cups], a pound and half of butter, three ounces of caraway-seeds, six eggs beat well, a quarter of ounce of cloves and mace beat together very fine [use ground spices and stir them together], a penny-worth of cinnamon beat [about 1 to 2 tablespoons ground], a pound of sugar, a penny-worth of rose water [1 to 2 tablespoons], a penny-worth of saffron [½ to 1 teaspoon, or a full pinch], a pint and a half of yeast [1 package], and a quart of milk; mix it all together, lightly with your hands thus: first boil your milk and butter, then skim off the butter, and mix with your flour and a little of the milk, stir the yeast into the rest and strain it, mix it with the flour, put in your seed and spice, rose water, saffron, sugar and eggs, beat it all up well with your hands lightly [you can use a mixer], and bake it in a hoop or pan [a tube pan or an 8-inch cake pan], but be sure to butter the pan well. It will take an hour and a half in a quick oven [1 hour in an oven preheated to 350 degrees – but if you're using cake pans, watch carefully and test for doneness after 35 minutes]. You may leave out the seed if you choose it, and I think it rather better without it [I agree – the caraway undermines the saffron flavor]; but that you may do as you like [a common way to end many old recipes, but to which I often feel like adding, "well, hey, thanks"]. This recipes makes 2 loaves.

Mrs. Glasse's cake is somewhat plain – if you can call anything cooked with saffron plain – but it is a very pretty thing, good with afternoon tea, or in the evening with a scoop (or two) of vanilla ice cream. For a more modern – and quite rich – version, scout out a copy of Elizabeth David's *English Bread and Yeast Cookery* (Viking, 1980). The recipe calls for 80 threads of saffron (and, as David recorded on more than one occasion, she probably actually counted them, but I would make do with what I would call an over-generous pinch – that is, as you pinch your fingers together in the threads, scoop together a bit more, enough to have some threads dangling from the bunch you've gathered), as well as 2 cups of heavy, or clotted, cream! I have made the cake for Christmas feasts and, later on, in the darkest days of winter, and it always – always – brings a sense of summer to those who taste it. I will not record it here, in the hopes that readers will search the book out – for this recipe and all the others that are included in the book, but also for the sheer pleasure of reading about the subject through David's far more superior steely prose.

Where saffron was truly put to use in England – and this, too, has to have been influenced by the continuing threat of the plague – it was as a medicine. As early as 1587, Rev. Harrison was noting in the *Holinshed Chronicles* that

> *(besides the manifold use that it hath in the kitchen and pastries, also in our cakes at bridals and thanksgivings of women) [saffron] is very profitably mingled with those medicines that we take.*

Apothecaries, doctors, and women harvesting the forest and fields for ingredients to heal their families considered saffron a powerful antidote to an incredibly long list of complaints. These included all manner of cancers, particularly of the abdomen, bladder, spleen, and stomach, but also of the brain, lungs, and cervix. Used both as a poultice and a wash, saffron was said to relieve the itchy and painful eruptions of measles, smallpox, syphilis, and gout. Consumptives often rested more comfortably after sipping a strong saffron soup. A tonic made with white wine and a good measure of saffron was a potent remedy for spasms. It was famous for strengthening the heart, refreshing the brain, and relieving the troubles of the soul and infamous for freeing women from what was often referred to in public and written text as female obstructions, but which were whispered about in private as unwanted pregnancies.

(There is disagreement among many writers as to whether the old abortion recipes that call for saffron really meant true saffron or a plant that is known in the country as *saffen*, which is a low-growing evergreen. Horse farmers have been quoted as allowing their mares to eat saffen when they didn't want foals [it was called "threepenny bit herb" because the dosage was the amount that covered a silver threepenny piece]. However, other sources – such as the herbal books of William Turner, John Gerard, and Culpepper and the medical writings of Thomas Sydenham, known as the English Hippocrates – speak quite precisely and openly of saffron being used to bring about abortions. For historical interest, I will relate the instructions they give, but I do so only with the sternest of warnings to all not to try it themselves. All of the authors give more or less the same instructions: to brew one teaspoon of powdered saffron in one pint of boiling water, let it cool, and then sip two fluid-ounce doses through the day. They also all agree that more than this amount in a single day – or several pints taken over several consecutive days – would cause not only the fetus to die but the woman as well.)

Medicinally, saffron was most often used as the Prozac of its day, invariably recommended to relieve melancholy – a rampant problem not only in England but also on the Continent, with many in the populace feeling that life was less than sweet. As one contemporary sufferer wrote, saffron's primary virtue was that it "pierceth to the heart, provoking laughter and merriment." Others, though, were concerned about it being prescribed too often and warned, as Gerard did in his *Herbal* that "too much using to it cutteth off sleep, through want whereof the head and sences are out of frame."

Still, a profusion of saffron treatments for depression were written down in everything from learned medical manuscripts to common household accounts, attesting to their popularity. A common home prescription comes from Mrs. Martha Bradley in *The British House-*

wife, or The Cook, Housekeeper's, and Gardiner's Companion (1756), a book of marvelous advice for running a proper eighteenth-century home:

A Course to Relieve Melancholy

1 quarts white wine
1 ounce elderflower
1 ounce ash keys
1 handful each of roman wormwood, centarry and hyssop
1 dram saffron

Add all the ingredients to the wine and let steep for two days. Then drink a small wine glass two times a day.

A more professional prescription was to make a tincture of saffron. A recipe for this, and the one that follows, were recorded in *The British Flora Medica, or a History of the Medicinal Plants of Great Britain* by Benjamin Herbert Barton (1835)

Take 1 ounce of saffron added to 15 ounces of proof spirit. Digest for seven days, and filter. An Exhilarant dose, from forty to sixty drops in a glass of water.

For children suffering the malaise, Syrup of Saffron was advised:

Take of saffron – ten drachms
Boiling water – one pint
Lump sugar – three pounds

Macerate the saffron in the water for twelve hours, in a vessel lightly covered; strain the liquid, and add the sugar.

Even the Countess of Kent in her *Rare and Select Secrets in Physicks and Cheruegy* (1659) sings the praise of saffron's relief of melancholy: "It is good to comfort the vitall spirits, passions trembling and pensiveness of the heart and helpeth all malignity oppressing it." She then provides the following elaborate instructions:

An Excellent Sirrup against Melancholly

Take

4 quarts juice of pearmint

8 quarts juice of buglofs

8 quarts juice of borrage

1 drachm of the best English saffron – bruise it and put it into the juice

then take

2 drachm of kerms, beaten to a powder and mix with the juices. Put in an earthenware vessel, cover or stop it for two days then drain and put into it:

1 pound of sugar to every quart of juice. Bring to a boil until a syrup is formed.

After it boils take

1 drachm of spice of dramber

2 drachm of *diamargariton frigidum* and suspend slenderly in a linen bag in the syrup. Bring again to a boil and add one or two teaspoons of honey to clarify. This will rise the scum and make the syrup clear. When the syrup is taken off the flame, add ¼ pint of juice of balm.

The Countess recommends a dosage of one spoonful in the morning and again at night for three days together.

There was no dearth of reasons why people found themselves so universally bereft, for these were tremulous times and saffron's fortunes in England rose and fell with the stability of the land. After the fairly sane reign of Elizabeth, there arrived the grasping, dangerous commands of James, the two Charleses, another James, and finally the cold – but somewhat reconciling – rule of William and Mary. Religion complicated everything; the discovery and conquering of new worlds intensified a certain sense of nationalistic dislocation that would only increase as the intellectual ferment of the Enlightenment approached.

In Saffron Walden, however, life continued on a fairly even keel, much as it had always done. Different sorts of people came and went – the Celts had come first, then the Romans, followed by Saxons who were occasionally enmeshed in Vikings who, every now and then, insisted that the town be part of the Danelaw. The motto of the constant native must have been similar to the one present-day Iowans have about their state weather, "If you don't like what you see, wait and it will change."

But the town itself was almost always a fair place to live, surrounded by fertile farmland and served well by the wise inclination of its inhabitants not to place their fortune all in one basket. Hard up against the saffron fields, there were barley fields to use in the town's malting and brewery concerns (by the early 1800s, there were over thirty of both), which found sufficient demand for beer from London to exist together without too much competition. The large marketplace in the center of town drew in the woolen trade, and there were enough weavers in the village that a leading bigwig worried aloud at a town meeting that the morals of the young women who manned the weaving looms would be corrupted by the high wages they received for their work.

These industries, along with the needs of the local farmers and the rare luck of its location – just far enough away from the coast and

London not to have ever been sacked or bombed in all the centuries of combats – assured that Saffron Walden remained intact and flourished. To this day, you can walk its winding, narrow streets and see mediaeval barns and Tudor homes – some patched and slightly altered but essentially the same sturdy little buildings they were when they were built hundreds of years ago.

And for many years it was even chic among the cosmopolitan crowd to take a jaunt up to Saffron Walden, where one's prestige was often recognized by a present of saffron. Town records relate that a whole pound of freshly made saffron was given to Anne, Lady Pagett, when she visited in 1546. Queen Elizabeth's attorney received a similar gift when he came to visit the Duke of Norfolk, who had taken up residence at the family home of his wife, Margaret Audley (who, as the daughter of Thomas Audley – the chancellor who served at the trial of Anne Boleyn – could *not* have been a favorite of Elizabeth's).

It was the Audley family, however, who truly made Saffron Walden a fashionable destination. When Margaret's son, Thomas Howard, inherited the estate, he decided to build a more commodious house for himself. Howard had been appointed by James I to be the Lord Chamberlain, then was made the Lord High Treasurer when he revealed a plan to blow up the king – and, for good measure, the Parliament – during the Gun Powder Plot. A fairly good-looking man, in spite of his gaunt lips and small, cynical eyes, Howard was said to have been extremely ambitious; vainglorious and given to ostentatious should have been added to his description as soon as his house – which he called Audley End – began to spread across the Saffron Walden horizon. He is recorded as explaining that he merely wished to provide the king and his court with a comfortable place to escape the pressures of London for a few days of peaceful hunting, but when the king finally saw the nearly completed house, he dryly observed that it was "too large for a king, but might do for a Lord Treasurer." James's unease – and possible gloomy suspicions that one of his favorites was toying with him – might have been relieved by Howard's gift of a pound and a quarter of saffron, but then here, too, was extravagance on display with the price of the king's saffron listed in the town's record as being four pounds sterling.

Audley End was completed in 1615, after nearly thirteen years of construction. It was, as James had recognized, much bigger than many of his own palaces, comprising three courtyards, thirty towers, and a grand total of 750 rooms.

Three years later, Howard was charged with embezzlement and corruption for accepting kickbacks and bribes. In harsher times, he would quickly have been beheaded, but these were more subtle days, and so it was deemed that he should be heavily fined. Gradually, the enormous upkeep of the colossal Audley End tightened around his neck and, added to the debt he owed the king, slowly strangled him to death.

Howard's family was left penniless for many years until Charles II came to visit in 1665 and found both the house and the neighborhood much to his taste. After graciously accepting a pound and a quarter of saffron spread out across a costly silver plate, the king decided to relieve the family of their burden and offered to buy the property for fifty thousand pounds. He gave the Howards thirty thousand pounds outright and arranged to pay the rest in dribs and drabs. Charles's high-spirited court made a great deal of fun at Audley End, and Saffron Walden itself realized a pretty penny or two from the noble crowds that tagged along whenever Charles took up residence. The king and his friends treated the town almost like a theme park of idyllic rural life; they rode and hunted, played party games in the garden, held sporting events in the courtyards. The homeless Howards, however, never saw another dime from Charles – or even his successor, William (though they seemed to have petitioned the new king as soon as he ascended the throne in 1689). When William came down to see his land, he was given the usual gift and, possibly because he was a foreigner and in an unfamiliar part of his new kingdom, he asked to see the saffron fields and be provided with some blossoms so he could examine them himself. His visit did not result in any further payments to the family, but twenty years later, right before he died, William decreed that Audley End should be given back to the Howards.

The last saffron present recorded in the town's roll was delivered to King George I in 1717. It was only a small amount of saffron, enough to pack a silver snuff box. George was also the last king to have stayed at Audley End when it was in its glory; nine years later, Henry Howard, the eighth earl of Suffolk, inherited the property and in a fit of practical economy had a big chunk of the house torn down.

Bit by bit, as Audley End passed from the Howards, to the Countess of Portsmouth, to Lord Braybrooke, the house shrank. By the time Capability Brown was commissioned to landscape the grounds, Audley End was but thirty impressive rooms – exhibiting a mere sliver of its former grandeur.

Just as Audley End dwindled, so too did the surrounding fields of saffron. In 1768, the botanist John Martyn lamented in his book *Flora Rustica* that saffron, "will probably soon be lost to this country, and we shall be wholly at the mercy of foreign dealers in this commodity; who sophisticate it with safflower, marygolds, etc., whereas our's comes out of the hands of the growers pure and genuine."

The Lord Braybrooke of 1790 took a tour of his neighborhood and declared he didn't find a single crocus blooming anywhere upon the land. He must not have peeked over any of the town's garden walls, because there were a few citizens who continued to grow some saffron out of sentiment for the old days or because it gladdened their hearts to see something blooming in the garden before the winter's first frost. Enough saffron remained in the town so that when the vogue to study nature seized well-brought-up men and women, visitors came in search of the flowers and were fond of picking them as souvenirs to take back home with them.

One such visitor would have been a Miss Elizabeth Blackwell, who, with the seeming encouragement of several well-connected London doctors, took as her life's work a complete study of England's herbs, entitled *A Curious Herbal, containing five hundred cuts of the most useful plants, which are now used in the practice of physick. Engraved on folio copper plates, after drawings taken from life* (1737). Filling two enormous volumes, the drawings are grouped in fours, each joined with a leaf of text. Each plant takes up a single page, executed in pen and ink with exquisitely subtle and careful detail. Underneath every drawing Miss Blackwell lists a concise but full description of each plant: the place it is likely to be found growing, what it is used for, and finally its name in different languages – starting, of course, with classical Greek and Latin, then followed by the countries where it is most common.

Miss Blackwell's artistic talent is captured not so much in her perfect rendering of leaf and flower (most women of a certain breeding and class were taught to draw as part of their general education, and even the least gifted achieved a basic degree of competence) as in the sense of character she imbues to her subject. Still, the sweetness of her work resides in the little bit of herself gleaming in these plates, seen in how the blossoms seem to lounge in sweet abandon and the way an array of very amiable bugs and insects crawl here and there across her patient sitters.

Miss Blackwell – and she *must* have been a Miss for all her commitment to her art (though I can't imagine her a very unhappy one; her dedication at the front of each volume lists far too many patrons, and every one a man, who helped her to complete her travels and assist in her studies for the woman to have been a lonely spinster, let alone a bitter old maid) – made her saffron entry a particularly beautiful one. The small flower arches delicately across the thick page, the black ink she drew it with – now a soft violet – almost the same color as the streak that runs down one of the petals. When she lists its uses, she mentions the usual ones (though she, too, referred to its unique usefulness to women). Her hand is neat and graceful, the result of a good tutor and endless practice. To paint such a portrait, she must have sat very still for a very long time. Maybe she walked across the old fields around Saffron Walden, visiting those that were still called by their former uses – Saffron Well Field; Saffron Gardens; Saffron Grounds, and the like – until she found one or two lone survivors. More likely, though, someone caught sight of her early one autumn morning peeping over their garden gate and invited her to come in. As the sun grew warm, the lady of the house would certainly have brought Miss Blackwell a glass of refreshment and, intrigued by her visitor's pursuit, would have lingered nearby, now and then regaling her with stories of how, not so long ago, everywhere you cast your eyes this time of year, the ground was carpeted with purple flowers and the fingertips of everyone you met were tinged a stubborn orange blush. Under her fashionable yet sensibly small bonnet (which shades her skin but does not block the light), the callus-hardened pad of her index finger, forever smudged with ink, the ebony style of her steel-tip drawing pen gnawed, even splintered, by her habit of biting it as she ponders the work before her – Miss Blackwell's head would be bent to concentrate on her task. She would not have heard very much of what her hostess said, though a part of her – the part schooled by the well-brought-up lady's mandatory attendance at dreary social engagements – would be tuned in just a little in case a polite response was necessary. The rest of her would be lost in unmasking the secret of her subject ("*Should I picture it at the brimming moment of its flowering, or closed, like the point of a sharp knife, piercing the ground and then, perhaps beneath, the bloom unfurling and the rigid chives pulsing at its center?*"), slowly deciphering saffron's beauty and longing – grasping – to capture the essential perfection of this adopted citizen of English soil.

Fare Thee Well

Croci are so confined to peculiar localities,
that a species may be easily so lost.

REVEREND WILLIAM HERBERT,
A History of the Species of Crocus, 1846

The one true thing that can be said about saffron is that it never wears out its welcome. When it is no longer wanted or appreciated, it simply withdraws from the landscape.

Shy was the term Reverend William Herbert, the Dean of Manchester, used when he described saffron's retiring nature. Crocuses were his life's work, a passion that left the souls of his faithful flock playing second fiddle as he wandered the world in the mid-1800s searching for every variance in shade and nuance the flower took. To explore the places he could not travel to, he enlisted a wide circle of friends, ambassadors, and foreign dignitaries, who seemed to have obliged him by setting aside official duties to tramp out into the countryside and hunt for native specimens, then send back a sample or two for him to grow in his greenhouse in the smog-darkened clatter of industrializing England. The Reverend compiled all of the information he had gathered over the years in a manuscript before he succumbed to illness and died (the preface of his posthumously published study tragically surmises that he might have picked something up on his treks, overlooking the fact that he was not a young man and that the heat and diligence of passionate pursuits – even one involving a mere flower – often ruin one's health). In his gentle, touching style, however, he writes quiet tenderly of saffron's modern peril.

"I suspect that the birthplace of C. *sativus* [saffron crocus], and many of its happy homes, has long [been] converted into vineyards."

Led by history books, rumor, and instinct, in places as close to home as Saffron Walden and as far away as Turkey, Herbert searched every autumn for sweeping vistas of purple blooms and found instead the land transformed, plowed under and usurped for more convenient uses. Cultivated saffron fields began to be plowed under across Europe toward the end of the seventeenth century and given over to the cultivation of discoveries brought back from the great ocean expeditions. Corn and potatoes quickly took to European soil and were found to be more expedient – and far less troublesome – to grow and harvest; the elite crowd's fashionable tables were now crammed with pots of chocolate, tea, and coffee, cakes fragrant with vanilla and citrus, and dizzying glasses of addictive liqueurs that the Medici queens of France insisted on serving at their courts. Outside of its far-away native homes, saffron's presence dwindled to those few places where the people could not see their lives without its sunny presence nor their feasts without the spice's spiny heat. The south of France, Spain, and Italy all happened to have warm climates where the corm, if it willed itself, would have certainly have grown on its own accord, but it didn't have to. The threads had embroidered themselves so expertly into the fanciful design of these lands that not only was it cosseted in well-tended fields, but its harvest became an occasion to celebrate, to fill the village plaza with one last whirling summer spree.

And here, in these few places, is where saffron would have remained, if not for the play of money and God that propelled it toward America. The journey began in the time of the Reformation – one of those periods in history when ordinary lives were routinely transformed overnight. On October 31, 1517, when Martin Luther tacked his thoughts on the doors of the Wittenberg castle cathedral, he fragmented the world into sharp shards. The spirit of Luther's beliefs had the effect of liberating the clergy, emboldening the peasants, and making everyone question the very rhythm of everyday life. And, as a result, more ways of worshiping the same God were brought into being than even Luther could have imagined or desired.

Consider, first, the Anabaptists, who came to believe that such an important thing as being baptized should be done with the careful heart and mind of an adult. That was their main disagreement not only with Rome but with Luther's teachings as well. Their disagreement with the secular state took the form of refusing to bear arms or take an oath. Then their leaders – particularly the charismatic and handsome young tailor John of Leiden – took those principles one step further and insisted that the world would be better off without civil laws, marriage, or private properties.

At this point, some Anabaptists thought the leaders had gone too far and turned instead to Menno Simons, a former Catholic priest. Simons wanted to turn Christianity back to the times of the apostles and so recognized the only two sacraments that Jesus himself was recorded as having performed – baptism and the transformation embodied in the Last Supper. His followers, who were found mainly in Switzerland and Germany, became known as Mennonites and distinguished themselves by attempting to live an uncomplicated life devoted to God and family. The Amish, centered mostly in Germany and led by Jacob Amman, broke off from the Mennonites and clung to an even more fundamental line, one that would separate itself entirely from the world and refrain from all outward displays of embellishment, even to the point of refusing to build churches.

To one degree or another, the modest beliefs of these good people so greatly rubbed against the rulers of the time that town squares across central Europe smoldered with great bonfires built with the kindling of unrecanting followers, their tortured bodies neatly tied and stacked together to carefully feed the flames. John of Leiden, who for a time took over the city of Münster and ruled it as the Kingdom of Zion, was clawed with hot pincers until his bones were exposed. His tongue was pulled from his mouth, and finally he was stabbed in the heart. Men were publicly castrated, eviscerated; women and children were tightly bound and thrown into the Danube and the Rhine. Even those who attempted to renounce their new faith were run down and executed.

Worst of all, the faithful's farmhouses were burned, their orchards cut down, their vines torn apart, and the ground seeded with salt so that nothing would ever grow there again. Of all the horrors the sects suffered, this was by far the most unbearable, for it struck to the quick, threatening values that were in form and substance older and more sacred than even Christianity – the divinity of the earth in sustaining life.

The Anabaptists had all but been destroyed in the siege of Münster, and the Mennonites and Amish, along with like-minded kin, decided to flee their homelands. They were joined by another persecuted sect, the German Dunkards, who in reverence to the Trinity plunged their believers three times into the baptismal water (but somehow became more famous for dipping their delicious donuts into their morning coffee – a secular spin on a display of piety, if ever there was one). Many found shelter in sympathetic England, but a few more adventurous souls (particularly the Dunkards) sailed straight for the American colonies when they heard of William Penn's vision for all religions to be able to live in tolerance together in what he called the "Holy Experiment" of a peaceable kingdom. In 1683, the Dunkards traveled to Pennsylvania and founded the village of Germantown just outside Philadelphia. With good reports coming back from America, the foreigners left England for settlements along the Hudson but, longing for a place of their own, soon turned toward Pennsylvania where they discovered the heart of God beating beneath the undulating hills of the Susquehanna River valley.

After all the Amish and Mennonites had been through, after all the miles they had traveled, it is easy to imagine how exhilarated they must have felt when they saw such promising country stretching before them. Here were forests of strong trees, filled with more game than they could ever possibly use, rimming endless fields of sweet and fertile virgin soil. Word spread to families left behind in Europe that Utopia had been found, and by the beginning of the Revolutionary War, the German, Swiss, and Alsatian people who composed the two religious communities and who were soon joined by their compatriots from Rhineland, Westphalia, and Saxony constituted a third of Pennsylvania's population. The English settlers began to refer to them all as the Dutch (though none have even a smidgen of Dutch ancestry), and if they did not exactly warm to their new neighbors with their different language, customs, and dress, the English came to enjoy the benefits of their hard work as their skillful farming fed the growing nation. Under the tenets of their faith, the Pennsylvania Dutch communities helped each other to construct handsome stone farmhouses and sturdy barns. They cleared wide swatches of forests and turned the river valley into a tawny mosaic of wheat, oat, and barley fields. Cherry and apple orchards padded the hillsides; neat beds of vegetables and herbs swelled in vast profusion to their wide kitchen doors.

And though they dressed in plain attire and led an austere life of work and prayer – as they still do even to this day, essentially living as they have always done in a freeze-frame of rural eighteenth century – there was nothing unadorned or the least bit restrained about the food they made. These were people who cooked – and loved to do so almost as much as they loved to eat, setting tables that swayed with a multitude of dishes, some plain, others in their way quite fancy, all packed with abundantly distinct flavors. The Pennsylvania Dutch settlers cooked in a style that was still touched by the Middle Ages – rich in spices, sharp with vinegar, mellow with honey. Many of their dishes were made in one pot and composed of varying flavors that, over a long and slow cooking period, melted into a pleasing, savory mélange. Travelers who passed through the region (which forms a diagonal slant from east to west across the lower quarter of the state) never forgot the meals they tasted there, especially at a tavern called the Sun Inn run by the evangelical Moravians in the small town of Bethlehem – possibly the country's first gastronomical destination. The meals that were offered at the inn – pots brimming with scrapple-stuffed pork belly and tart sauerbraten; platters laden with baked trout or roasted duck; bowls of fresh vegetable pickles and succotash; rich, sugary, creamy pies; cakes as tall and airy as starched lace bonnets; baskets of dense, chewy breads; and everything washed down with pitchers of root beer, ginger beer, buttermilk, apple cider, mulberry wine – were the same as those cooked in farmhouses, and the descriptions of them that can be read in old letters and diaries sound as delicious now as they must have been then.

It was hard, though, in the new country, to find the necessary ingredients. The Pennsylvania Dutch incorporated many native foods into their recipes, but some ingredients had no acceptable substitutes, and these, such as spelt, a highly nutritious grain known as German wheat, were brought from Europe. One old legend, traced to the batter of a delicious cake, has it that saffron first came to America packed in the trunk of yet another religious group, called the Schwenkfelders. Many of the sect members had grown saffron in Germany as a cash crop and saw no reason to leave their livelihood behind when they emigrated. If they did, then others soon followed suit, for by 1730 enough farms were growing saffron across the region to meter out a small yet steady supply that satisfied the local cooking needs.

But it was a couple of German Jewish merchants in Philadelphia who realized that there was money to be made in the local crop if they could offer saffron to the Spanish colonists stuck on Caribbean islands without a single pinch to alleviate their homesickness. The venture had much in its favor: the merchants had experienced farmers eager to grow saffron and sailing ships that could make the voyage faster down the American coastline than across the Atlantic Ocean. They also had in place a network of Quaker and Jewish merchants on the islands who could readily provide agents to trade and sell the threads. Even though Pennsylvania's climate is not ideal for growing saffron, the able Dutch farmers managed to coax the corms into bloom year after year. It was a small matter, then, to increase production and ship the harvest down to the Philadelphia docks and pack it into cargo holds alongside molasses, rum, cod – and, far too often, slaves. The venture was a success almost from the start. In the years before the Revolutionary War, saffron was listed on the Philadelphia commodity exchange on nearly a weekly bases, its price calculated the same as it had always been – equal to gold.

The American saffron trade would have continued swimmingly enough if the War of 1812 hadn't intruded. British blockades jammed ports, sunk merchant ships without mercy, and left the saffron farmers in Pennsylvania with a heap of threads on their hands. Since trade with the Spanish islanders (who had their own problems with the British) was never fully reestablished after the war, this would have been the end of American saffron except that the thrifty Pennsylvania Dutch cooks took to adding even more of it to their dishes.

When I began to spend a great deal of my time thinking about food, I kept smacking up against the undertone of dismay – even disdain – that many writers use when exploring the subject of American cooking. I kept thinking at first (as I usually do) that there was something I was obviously missing here, some intellectual thread – and probably taste – that I was lacking, for the truth of the matter is that there isn't much in American cooking – past or present – that I find wanting. Over the years I might even have grown to be a little more pig-headed about the matter, but I realize now that I have this firm underlining of good will toward our nation's cooking because I was raised in such close proximity to the Pennsylvania Dutch. My sympathies were helped, of course, by my having been being born into a family of good, even excellent, cooks, but much of my compassion is the direct result of the lazy Sunday drives my father took his family on.

After Mass (and a hardy breakfast of scrambled eggs and scrapple – a sort of Pennsylvania Dutch pâté of ground pork scraps, cornmeal, and spices that is sliced and fried until a crisp shell forms), still in our starched, petticoated dresses and clean shirts, we would pile into the car. Destinations were always murky, though they must have been discussed between my parents because it was nearly impossible to lead my mother blindly where she would not go. But the information rarely filtered down to my brother and sister and me before – and even after – we climbed into the backseat. We must have complained, or at least whined; there was surely some pinching and squabbling about seat hogging and who would be squeezed into the middle, but it never stopped the Sunday trips or even cut them noticeably short – a feat that I marvel at now that I am the parent of two sweetly obstreperous children of my own.

With all the propaganda power of hindsight and memory, I know I see these excursions as the best of times, free of our family's particular woes, and more open to the wonders of the world than we could ever have been aware of, yet the truth of the matter is that the knowledge I hold most dear was learned squeezed in between Joe and Sue, and in trusting that our parents were driving us someplace good. If there was anything happening in center city – a new exhibit at the museums, perhaps, or at the convention center (the boat show, despite the fact that our family would never have imagined owning a boat, was a yearly favorite) – we would head down the East River Drive and into town. Other times we just drove, away from our crowded Philadelphia neighborhood, across the Schuylkill River and through Conshohocken to a highway that would soon peter out into a two-lane country road leading into the bosom of Lancaster County.

This was a different world, not so much for the people that we zoomed past hobbling along in old-fashioned black buggies and wagons drawn by side-blinded horses, but for the wide-open stateliness of the land, the horizon stretching for all eternity, unimpeded by anything taller than a tree, so unlike our constricting city. Sometimes we would stop at a roadside farm stall or market to buy some vegetables or a basket of berries; if it was the fall or late spring, we headed for one of the numerous fairs that still dot the county and compete for tourist business. The handiwork on display – perfect pies and well-turned blanket stitching – allowed my mother to fall into easy conversation with the women in gossamer bonnets, their long dresses covered with clean aprons making them appear like more approachable versions of the nuns I spent all my youth seated in uneasy attention before. But my father had a harder time with the men who seemed to be more standoffish, even forbidding, in their black garb, the elders with their long beards, and the boys and young men, too, masked by a watchful demeanor. As a rule, and generally to his children's embarrassment, my father rarely hesitated to engage strangers in conversation, particularly in a place he didn't know anything about. All kinds of people, from every walk of life, fell into step with him and allowed him to ask sometimes rather pointed questions about their lives. Yet he rarely approached the Amish and Mennonite men. Or, if he did, it was for something as general as directions, and then he met them with a polite reserve of his own.

And so the afternoon passed in wandering down country roads into small, clapboard towns where a different language was spoken and another way of life was lived. We rambled across farms where the families opened their doors to strangers and showed them how it was possible to get along without electricity and modern appliances. We marveled over displays of quilts and handsomely crafted furniture. We hung on split-rail fences to pet placid cows and stare at gigantic pigs. Horses took sugar cubes and apples from our outstretched hands; chickens and roosters pecked about our feet. We did everything that we possibly could do in an afternoon in the country, and then we got back into the car and went looking for someplace to eat.

This was, I suspect, the real reason why my father drove us out this way as often as he did. He was not a man given to gastronomical fantasies. In fact, he greatly annoyed my mother with his lack of any clear desire for food. "Why bother?" she'd say in later years when it was just the two of them to cook for. Yet her own fine appetite and genuine need to cook would get the better of her, and she would force herself to make them a dinner she knew he would only pick through but she would enjoy without bounds. My father, however, held a special hankering for everything prepared by the Pennsylvania Dutch. I don't know where this came from; his mother was born in Ireland, his father from Protestant English stock (a shame he tried to hide by insisting that the family's name was really Welsh), but he would dig into a platter of stewed pigs' feet or a bowl of spelt soup and swear he was in heaven. The places where we ate were known as family-style restaurants, where there was no such thing as an individual order. Rather, the serving dishes were set out on the table and everyone helped themselves. There was always freshly baked bread and an assortment of side dishes (the traditional accompaniment of seven sweet and seven sour relishes). The places where my brother and sister and I most wanted to go to were the ones that placed whole cakes and pies down along with the main meal. Sometimes we shared a long table with other families, but it didn't matter at all who we were with. The food was so good and plentiful and we ate so hungrily ("Better a burst stomach than wasted food" a placard read at one establishment) that we hardly ever talked even among ourselves. Instead we put our hearts and minds to the task at hand, ate all that we could possibly hold, then waddled out to the car and we drove back home in the falling dusk, satiated with our Sunday drive.

There, among the artful dishes of the Pennsylvania Dutch, I first became familiar with saffron. I can remember only the look of it, though – how it soaked the noodles in a golden shade, roused a slice of chicken, and powdered the plump belly of a trout – but I cannot recall ever tasting it before that time in the cold northern city. It is conceivable that I was too young to be astonished by such a voluptuously natural flavor; children are rarely amazed at such earthy pleasures, taking them as a matter of course and being guided instead by their own natural inclination to either embrace or shy away. I do know, though, by the recollection of my mother's small reprimanding smack on my arm, that I sucked up the noodles with a lusty slurp because they were plump with sweet butter, chewy but soft, like creamy eggs. But, then, my memory of those essentially simple meals, where much of what is good in American cooking can be found, are all accompanied by such sounds of gluttony.

Saffron is still grown in and around Lancaster County, though hardly any of it makes it out into the world, and what does travels only as far as the Reading Terminal Market in Philadelphia. American saffron does not have the elegant languor of its European and Eastern cousins. It is more bumptious – tasting of the earth, its color diffusing more freely into the hue of a broiling morning sunrise. Maybe it is the dark, rich Pennsylvania dirt, or the too-short burst of steaming hot days followed by the bracing northern chill. Or maybe it is just the shortness of time, the freshness of the stock, that like the country's cooking itself gives our saffron the raucous radiance of a teenager only beginning to grasp the full expanse of God's gifts.

Schwenkfelder Cake

As I have said, there are conflicting reports about the Schwenkfelders. Either they're blood relatives who were saffron farmers in Germany, or they were a conservative religious sect founded by Kasper Schwenkfelder, whom Luther suspected of harboring some Anabaptist leanings. Whatever the case may be (and I'll throw my hat in with the latter theory), the Schwenkfelders loved saffron and brought corms and a whole style of saffron cooking with them when they came looking for refuge on America's shores.

This cake succeeded in crossing over from being a regional specialty to a staple of American cooking, and the recipe for it used to be included in most general American cookbooks. It is simply a delicious cake, but what probably made it a favorite is its versatility. Today it might be considered a breakfast or coffee cake, but I have seen it specifically mentioned for after dinner, as a late-night snack, and (in a 1950s-era cookbook) as a "teen party favorite."

The saffron flavor in the cake is very light but unmistakable, and it's quite lovely with the cinnamon-brown sugar topping. For a special treat, lightly toast a slice and then top it with some ice cream.

For the cake:
2 medium potatoes, peeled and boiled until tender
½ cup of water from boiling potatoes
a medium-sized pinch of saffron
1 package dry yeast
1 cup and ¼ teaspoon sugar
¾ cup warm milk
1 stick of butter
2 large eggs, slightly beaten
5 cups all-purpose flour

For the topping:
1 cup all-purpose flour
1 teaspoon cinnamon
1 cup brown sugar, firmly packed
1 stick butter, chilled
2 tablespoons very soft butter

Preheat oven to 350 degrees.

To make the cake: Mash the potatoes well, making sure there are no lumps left, and reserve. In a small saucepan, bring ¼ cup of the potato water to boil, remove from heat, and stir in the saffron. Let steep for 20 minutes.

In a small bowl, mix the rest of the potato water with the yeast and ¼ teaspoon of sugar. Stir until the yeast and sugar are dissolved. Let stand in a warm place until the yeast starts to bubble.

In a large mixing bowl, stir together the warm milk, butter, eggs, and the rest of the sugar. Add 3 cups of flour and stir to combine. Add the mashed potatoes and the yeast mixture to the flour mixture. Stir again just until all the ingredients are incorporated. With a metal spoon, mix in the saffron water and the rest of the flour. The dough will be pretty stiff.

Turn the dough out onto a floured surface and knead for 5 to 10 minutes, or until the dough is silky and elastic. Transfer the dough to a well-greased bowl and turn it once to coat the surface of the dough with butter; then cover with a cloth and place the bowl in a warm place until the dough doubles in bulk – about 1 hour.

Punch down the dough and divide it in half; pat each half into a round shape. Place each half in a 9-inch layer cake pan and let rise again in a warm place until the dough doubles in size – about 30 to 45 minutes.

To make the topping: While the dough rises combine the flour with the cinnamon and brown sugar in a medium-sized bowl, and with a fork or pastry knife, or your fingertips, work the chilled butter into the dry ingredients until it looks like bran flakes. When the dough has doubled in size again, brush the warm butter over the top of each cake, completely covering the surface; then sprinkle the topping equally over the butter on each cake.

Bake for 30 to 35 minutes, or until the tops are brown. Remove from the pans and cool on a cake rack.

Saffron Noodles

I have copied this recipe from a wonderful cookbook by William Woys Weaver called Pennsylvania Dutch Country Cooking *(Abbeville Press,*

1993). Weaver is a leading authority on Pennsylvania Dutch cooking, and he recommends grinding saffron threads with a mortar and pestle before beginning this recipe.

4 teaspoons cold butter
1 cups all-purpose flour
⅛ teaspoon salt
2 large egg yolks
¼ teaspoon ground saffron (see above)

Cut the butter into the flour and salt to form fine crumbs. Beat the eggs and egg yolks together until lemony; then add the saffron. Let the eggs rest a little bit for the saffron color to rise (about 15 minutes – because the eggs are cold, the saffron won't really blossom in color and flavor the way it would in a watery hot liquid).

Make a well in the center of the crumb mixture and add the eggs in one swoop. Work together until you have a dough. On a lightly floured surface, roll out the dough as thin as possible, or run it through a pasta maker, then drape it over a clothesline or the back of a chair (I use a cupboard door). Let the dough dry for about 20 minutes; then lay the dough on a flat surface and cut it into thin strips. You can leave the noodles long or cut them short.

Bring a large pot of salted water to boil and drop the noodles in. Bring the water back to a boil and cook no more than 4 minutes. Drain quickly and mix in big pats of sweet butter. Serve and eat immediately. Serves about 6.

Fiesta de la Rosa del Azafran

Can we ever have too much of a good thing?

MIGUEL DE CERVANTES, *Don Quixote de la Mancha*, 1605

I.

There are bits and pieces of many cultures remaining in Consuegra today. But when the bus crossed over the little stone bridge and pulled to the side of the road before a bar to let me and an elderly couple off, I recognized nothing but an awfully small village in the middle of nowhere. A few weeks before, I had heard about Consuegra's saffron festival, which is held each year on the last weekend in October, when the flowers have all been picked and almost all the threads have been harvested. There would be a festival queen, called the Dulcinea in honor of Cervantes' not-so-delusional hero, who saw a dragon in the windmills that still stretch across the hill below the town's castle. At the festival, I thought, there would be dancing and music, perhaps some food, and wine I hoped, but surely there would have to be saffron – pure and fresh, enough to stir the air with its bracing scent. And so, somehow, I got an airplane ticket and a few dollars together, kissed my startled family good-bye, and took myself off to a country I had never been to and whose language I did not speak, my eyes dazzled by an imagined vista stippled in a violet haze.

It was around three o'clock in the afternoon when I arrived, and all the shops were shuttered; the elderly couple were quickly picked up by a relative, and I was left out on the street with no idea of where to find the hotel. Two policemen happened by and the one who recognized the name of the hotel shook his head and waved his hands enough to make me understand that it was far away – too far to walk. They had nothing else to do and were amenable to driving me in their police van through the deserted streets, back over the bridge, and to the edge of town – actually a yard or so beyond the town – on the narrow shoulder of the two-lane highway. The hotel, the police assured me, was hidden across the street behind a screen of scrub trees. I thanked them and crossed the lonely road to find, indeed, a dusty lot filled with cars and an old blue bus before a long white building with a red tiled roof and a deeply shaded porch. A Coke machine stood as a glaring sentry at the door. Chickens clucked behind a wooden fence; flocks of small birds rustled through the heavy weave of thorn bushes near the steps. Inside the hotel, a light nattering of voices filtered through the cool, empty vestibule. If the festival were to begin that night, I thought, wouldn't there be more people here, filling the town and the hotel? Perhaps I was early, or maybe I was wrong. All day long, from the moment I got off the plane in Melagra, and then Madrid, and made my bumbling and faltering way by bus through the magnificent vision of Toledo and now to this forsaken little spot, I had felt slightly lost, unable to make myself understood except to a few patient souls. A woman of a certain age – definitely beyond her student years – without a companion and taller – so very much *taller* – than women (and even men, it appeared) were made in this country, I was becoming convinced, down to my tired, jet-lagged soul, that it was possible that I could be very wrong about many things on this trip, from the location of the festival to its timing, to my need to be anywhere else but home. All of which gave way to the possibility that I could be stranded here in a clearly vacant hotel.

But I went ahead through the swinging doors at the end of the vestibule, where the voices seemed to be, and found a pleasing barroom with wide booths under the windows, a row of tables down the center, and a pool table at the back. A portly man behind the bar glanced curiously up at me as I approached but went back to his tallying of the previous evening's receipts when I stopped before him.

"Por favor," I mangled. "La fesitival del azafran."

His gray eyebrows shuttered a bit against my tortured pronunciation. He answered by turning away to call impatiently to a young man down at the other end of the bar. They talked among themselves, paused to eye me, I sensed, as a potentially bothersome situation. They must have decided on a course of action, for the young man disappeared through a door behind the bar while the older man took his books and pieces of paper away to its far end. The younger man soon returned with yet another young man who was dressed in a chef's white jacket and carefully wiped his hands on a cloth towel. In halting English, the chef asked me what I wanted. I gave him a piece of paper confirming the reservation that was made for me at home. After deciphering it, he announced me as the American guest and then returned to the kitchen. The young man left behind took a key tied to a block of wood that was hanging from the wall behind the liquor bottles and beckoned me to follow him. He led me through a beaded curtain, across a red-tiled patio roofed by a heavy grapevine, and up a wide flight of stairs to a dark hallway along which were grouped the hotel's rooms. He opened a door in the middle of the hall, gave me the key, and politely retreated while I went into the room. Shaded by closed metal shutters and furnished with two long narrow beds covered with frilly pink bedspreads, it was small and immaculate. For the moment, it didn't matter whether I was lost or not; here was a resting place where I could gather myself together. I locked the door, took off my clothes, and stood under the shower for a long time to wash away the grit of travel. Afterward, wrapped in a towel, I lay down on one of the beds. As the edges of the mattress rose to fold around me, yielding sleep, I heard the birds quivering in the bushes beneath the window and – from the gas station across the road – a faintly disco version of "Sympathy for the Devil."

It was six o'clock when I struggled from my stupor, dressed, and stumbled outside to find the town again. If this was indeed the weekend of the festival, I would be missing much if I did not hurry. Across the road and picketing the top of the distant hill were the windmills; the castle appeared as a worn bump at the very tip of the ridge. The road that led toward them was narrow, bordered by a rubble-strewn field dissected by a well-trampled footpath. A woman wearing a gaily printed apron over a black dress carried a large bouquet of flowers toward the white monuments marking the local cemetery. On the other side of the road, behind a row of garages and a large metal tower where the locally made wine was stored, a few modern houses appeared to have been recently constructed. In just a short block or two, however, older houses surfaced – finely kept with handsome wooden doors or heavy striped curtains hanging across their entrance.

The street became narrower and then suddenly opened up into a small plaza and spilled into a larger avenue. At the junction, I found a toy store full of mechanical dolls and circus dogs and a newspaper shop whose window was filled with movie stars on glossy magazine covers. Across the way was an entrance to a dusty park where old men in tightly buttoned sweaters and suit jackets, their caps pushed back upon their heads, exposing small, generously weathered, ruddy faces, sat together among beds of late-blooming roses. Before an enormous medieval church whose walls were pocked with age and possibly battles, street vendors from Senegal shouted out the wares spread at their feet on blankets – cheap umbrellas, scarves, packs of batteries, and knockoffs of designer handbags – the same things their compatriots offered in New York but somehow seeming more appealing, even unique, in the pale dust of this old church square. Children tugged at the hands and legs of the parents who stopped to look at the merchants' displays. They wanted to go on into the park along the riverbank, where roustabouts were assembling carousels and bumper cars and plain trees strung with bright incandescent bulbs burned in the depleting light like sparking embers among the dark leaves.

I crossed the bridge above the ghost of a river, a pale shadow of the one that rose up late one night in 1891 to rip apart half the town and whisk away four hundred lives. Beneath the pretty humpback bridge, not big enough to hold two cars at the same time, the wide old river bed is broken in two by a small cement channel dampened by a trickle of sluggish water. The rest of the river is now restrained miles away by dams and irrigation channels.

For a moment, I lingered on the bridge and thought about traveling out to find the rest of the river to see what it was like before. On these hardened plains, even beyond the advantage given by the high land, the river would have been the reason people stayed, why they found this a suitable spot to live. The very flatness of the land dictates the severe seesawing climate – the ground lies open and vulnerable, punished by the harsh winds of winter and the brooding heat of summer. Trees are scarce; water is scarcer. But this river must have spoken deep promises to generations past, allowing them to see a future far beyond their momentary existence. For that reason the whisper it made now seemed all the more piteous. What flowed below would not be enough to quench an evening's thirst, let alone inspire the fledgling dreams of a new life.

But it was growing late, and I needed to get up the hill to the windmill where the tourist office was to find out, I hoped, about the festival and to find someone who could speak English. I dashed into the tight coil of streets at the center of town, which were shadowed by the crush of old buildings whose tilting upper stories seemed to form a tunnel leading traffic into the light of the town's main square – the Plaza Mayor. For the moment I ignored the splendor of the square's finely designed municipal buildings, its elegant paving and graceful planting of bitter orange and fir trees. Instead, I continued scurrying up the increasingly steep streets until the town was brought to a halt by the sharp slope of the hill itself. Stone steps had been forged into the ground – worn and beveling, meandering up and up, leaving the town behind as if in pursuit of the retaining wall at the base of the windmills.

There are eleven restored windmills (and two others still in ruins) in Consuegra. Strung across the lower ridge of the hill, their whitewashed walls reflect the last of the day's heat, and their timbered spoke and four sails – locked and tied now – creak restlessly in the twilight's gathering wind. For the tourist trade, each windmill has the name of a character from Don Quixote painted above the door lintel. At the one named for Bolero, I found several students manning the tourist office, and except for a few disconnected words, none of them spoke English. Still, they managed to assure me about the festival – all of them, in fact, were home from universities in Toledo and Madrid to help with the weekend's events. Tonight, one of them managed to communicate to me through accomplished pantomime and drawings on a slip of paper, was the Dulcinea's debut; tomorrow local dishes made with saffron would be cooked in the park, and later there would be a saffron-picking contest and the starting of the windmill. Sunday, the Plaza Mayor would be the setting for the saffron-picking finals and a dance competition between neighboring towns. The students pressed into my hands brochures and leaflets, a map of the town, the festival booklet, and a souvenir poster, and I went out the door, glad that I had gotten the festival's date right but somehow not about anything more.

The day was rapidly dimming, casting long cobalt shadows across the far ridge of hills darkened with olive groves and grapevines. I turned in all directions, shading my eyes against the final shafts of sun cutting through the high clouds, but I saw no evidence of saffron, no purple stain creeping along the ground. Perhaps the harvest was all in, perhaps there were only the leaves, as thin and pointed as spears, lying trampled in the dirt. All could have been gathered and much of it could at this very moment be filling the town for the festival. The sound of guitars and drums, a woman's high yell followed by claps and shouts, drifted aloft from the valley. I was in need of a steadying glass of wine and the Dulcinea would be making her first appearance. I quickly picked my way back down the precipitous stairs and into town.

The plaza was crowded with people standing on benches and planters to catch a glimpse of the seventeen-year-old Dulcinea in her simple medieval gown draped with a wide ceremonial ribbon, her dark hair entwined with ropes of pearl. Her court, made up of seven teenage girls in the local costume of long paisley shawls and black and red dirndl skirts, followed behind the Dulcinea as the mayor in his very best pinstriped suit led her from the plaza through the main market street to the promenade along the river. Decorative arches blazing with red, yellow, and white lights were strung between the trees. The latest tractor models – a silver Lamborghini, a green Peugeot – were parked along the bank, ready to be shown off at the tractor pull in the morning. On the opposite side of the walk, booths displayed local products – cured meats, sausages, olive oil, beans, embroidered tablecloths, and fine lace.

I inched inside a crammed bar beside the park and pointed to a bottle of red wine and several plates of tapas for the bartender to give me, not knowing, or caring much, what it was I was ordering. After I paid, I carried my meal and glass to an outside table where I could watch the events. The Dulcinea was a pretty girl made beautiful by her role, her youthful grace a splendid foil against the preening manner of the officious mayor. Her court was better off than she; they did not have to parrot the Dulcinea's queenly composure and were free to enjoy their sudden celebrity. They sauntered gaily behind her, waving at classmates and giggling at the Japanese television crew who made them stop and walk toward their cameras again and again.

I sipped my wine and was content to eat the simple plate of sausage and beans, the two pieces of bread dipped in anchovy butter and then fried until crisp, and the smooth croquette of salted cod that would be my evening meal. It had grown remarkably dark by the time I finished; without the high-intensity glare of American streetlamps it was startling to realize how quickly darkness fell, how swiftly buildings and roads became masked in shadows. The Dulcinea was no longer in sight, and tired parents were carting sleeping children in their arms. Few people were on the bridge, and fewer still were on the street leading from the town. The further I went, the fuller night became. There was no moon, and the stars spreading across the endless sky were too distant, too dim, to even pick out the white monuments in the cemetery across the barren field. Somewhere I had taken a wrong turn, for a while I wandered about lost among shuttered houses until some children discovered me and went off to get their father, who came out of his house buttoning up his shirt and gesturing for me to get into his car. The children in the backseat laughed at the adventure of taking a strange woman to the hotel, but the father looked tired, only doing his duty. He pulled into the gas station and I got out, waving to the children who screamed and hollered *buenas noches!* out the windows, their singing voices streaming back to me long after they had disappeared down the dark road.

II.

He came up to where I sat in the Plaza Mayor, a courtly old man dressed in a formal gray suit. The skin of his face was pulled taut with age, cured by year after year in the vigorous sun. He had a winsomely large hooked nose and soft plump lips, which women must have found alluring when he was in his prime. His hair was still thick and mostly black, neatly combed back upon his perfectly round head.

What a strange little man, I thought, as I watched him approach, not realizing that what he was saying was meant for me. I had been up for hours wandering through the town. Already I had climbed to the castle, a ruined pile of stones in the midst of reconstruction, although even in its broken-down state its former grandeur was evident. While morning broke across the surrounding countryside, I stood at the topmost rampart trying to imagine the fever that would drive a man to gallop across the flat terrain knowing that the Moors were watching from these towers. For years, they stood along the battlement's walls, armed with the will of Allah, swift arrows, and heavy swords and watched the shimmer of heat and frost play across the flat terrain, knowing that someday someone would appear to proclaim this land for Christ.

"Thrust, my horsemen, for the love of the Creator!" El Cid implored his legions before the charge up the hill. "I am Ruy Díaz of Bivar, the chief, the brave one!"

Speed would have been their only cover; El Cid's soldiers must have whipped their horses into a furious stampede and stretched their bodies flat against the animals' necks to break the wind and shield themselves from the Moors' lethal arrows. On up the hill they stormed in one enormous wave, the snort of the horses, the drum of their hooves, the horrific warrior scream that leaped from the Spaniards' throats – all rolled down the hillside to saturate the valley and the small village below in a shuttering terror. Over the next one hundred years, Consuegra was won and lost, won and lost once more and then, in 1183, finally won by the Spaniards for keeps when the castle was presented in gratitude by the victorious King Alfonso VIII to the knights of the Order de San Juan de Jerusalem.

From the castle, I traveled down the bending road to each windmill, then hopped down the stone steps and found a small church where I could rest for a spell in a back pew. Built in the eighteenth century and dedicated to the town's patron, the Infant of Vera-Cruz, the church's intimate interior was illuminated by the brilliance of its Baroque detail. A few devotional candles before holy images of the saints flickered in the cool darkness. A life-size figure of Jesus Christ hung above the alter on an enormous gold filigree cross, his loins covered by a startlingly festive lime green couture-worthy brocade skirt. An old man dozed in a pew near the side alter, his breathing heavy and liquid, punctuated by tiny snorts that roused him to a startled consciousness. I left just as a young girl came rushing in – his granddaughter, perhaps, sent to find him, for after crossing herself with holy water and lighting a candle before a statue of the Virgin, she sat behind him and gently righted the cap that had slipped down his head and hovered a bit off his ear.

There were only a few people in the plaza by the time I got there – women rushing to do the morning shopping, a young father with his toddler son. I took a seat nearby to go through the brochures the students at the tourist office had given me the night before to try to decipher the day's events, when the strange little man hastened toward me, his arms waving wildly. When he stopped before me, the air about us grew heady with his sweet lemony musk, and as he rapidly uttered incomprehensible words I watched his full lips become dewy. The man paused in his speech only to extend his hand for me to shake, then launched off again until he realized with a start that I could not understand him at all. He switched to pantomiming, raising his hand to his mouth and pointing toward the river, then tapping his watch, the hands of which were approaching the noon hour.

"Va al parque," he remarked with great urgency and repeated the funny little eating motion. So I got up and hurried toward the park and the fairground, following the small crowd past the old church and the starkly modern colossal statue of El Cid that faces the castle's hill as if still contemplating his battle plan.

Here in the dirt under the autumn-tinged plain trees, people had set up tables, ignited small bonfires, and busily engaged in the competition for the best saffron dish. Some of the celebrants decorated their tables with handsome baskets of saffron blossoms, bowls of olives, garlic braids, and bottles of wine. Others had only the basket in which they had transported their ingredients and utensils sitting on the ground before their fire. Great stacks of kindling and chopped logs were piled on the side of each site; the smoke was pungently acidic with grape and oak twigs mixed with the sweet syrup of cherry and apple wood. Over the flames, most participants had placed iron tripods holding wide-bottomed pans with sloping walls – huge paella pans, though not everyone was making paella. Some were stirring the local dish composed of rough bread crumbs, sausages, garlic, tomatoes, and saffron, moistened with water or white wine. Others were preparing *gallina pepitoria,* a regional dish often served at weddings that requires a chicken somewhat past her fertile years, along with slivers of hard-boiled eggs, pine nuts, and ham. On the perimeter of a few fires were beans in tall clay pots. Some stirred a thick rice stew with long metal spoons, and, yes, here were a couple of bubbling paellas. One version, with an obvious eye on wowing the judges, was brimming with small crayfish, but the rest were the traditional mixture of chicken, rabbit, and sausage, some made fiery with long red peppers, but all (with varying degrees of pinches) redolent of saffron.

There were a few quite serious gentlemen – countrymen with thick hands scarred from their life of labor. The patience that is required of farming showed in the unhurried, casual rhythm of their cooking. But most of the contestants were formidable, bustling women who wore their contest numbers fastened with clothespins to the bibs of their floral aprons. The participants who had the most fun of all, however, were the five young brothers who were drinking the wine they were supposed to be pouring into their entry. When their number was called to present their dish to the judges (composed of a television personality from Madrid, local dignitaries, and a cooking teacher), the brothers organized a little parade, complete with flag waving and bottle tossing. The audience cheered them on, while the judges unsuccessfully tried to maintain their official composure. After much joking and fumbling, their dish was tasted and judged sublime, at which point the brothers felt compelled to fervently kiss the judges – men and women alike – to the rousing approval of everyone in the park.

Someone passed out forks and little cups, and the crowd that was growing by the minute with people who had traveled down from the cities for a day in the countryside pressed urgently forward toward the fires. They swarmed from pot to pot, hungrily forking or scooping up into their cups whatever they could manage. The little I got – the drunken brothers' dry mélange of bread crumbs and sausage, the chicken dish, and a bit of one paella – were all dense with the smoky flavor of the fires, the oily, robust local sausages, the subtle astringent nature of the crocus threads.

I took all that I could get, as well as a cup of red wine snagged from a man who stood over his fire stirring his dish with a long wooden paddle and ignoring the cooking advice of his friends sitting on top of the firewood behind him. By then I wanted to find a quiet place beside the river to eat. I had missed the tractor pull and the first dancing exhibition; at four there was the initial round of the saffron-picking contest, followed quickly by the grinding of the wheat at the mill. Two weary-looking gray-white ponies from the carnival rides grazed lazily on the grass growing in the dried riverbed below, and on the opposite bank the strange man who had urged me to the cooking contest was marching down the promenade, herding people together with his outstretched arms and the force of his personality. Most everyone else seemed to be headed off to find a place to rest for the afternoon. They wandered into nearby bars and restaurants; some stretched out on clothes spread across the dirt under the trees. A farmer and his family gathered around a haystack near where their comely goat was tied and ate what remained in the wide paella pan that the wife had made for the competition.

When I was finished eating, I took myself back across the bridge. I had heard in the hotel that morning as I sat and ate the breakfast that was offered me – two pieces of thick toast and a pot of bitter orange marmalade, washed down with a large hot cup of creamy chocolate – that in a house on the road leading out of town the last farmer to grow saffron in the area would have his wife sitting in the doorway picking the threads from the blossoms. I knew I would never be able to ask him all the questions I had – What had happened to the other saffron fields? Why did people stop growing the flower? How hard were the threads to pluck? But I wanted to find him anyway, if only to see his wife and maybe get a chance to sit with her and pull some threads myself.

As I wandered back up the hill, following the curve of the old Roman streets, I thought about what the Greek historian Strabo had written about the time after the final battle of the Punic War, when Rome began to secure the rest of Carthage's possessions, including the Iberian peninsula, for themselves. Legions of seasoned Roman soldiers scurried down through Gaul and across the Mediterranean Sea. They thought this would be a short, easy campaign, never suspecting the sort of frenzied resistance the natives would show. The Spaniards they encountered here were the descendants of Iberians who had been pushed up from the coast by the Carthaginian Phoenicians and became assimilated with the native tribes of Celtic origin who had claimed the plateau centuries before. These people were demons on horseback, passionate in their attacks. Even the women took up arms, and when they saw their towns and villages falling under Roman command, they took to slaughtering their own children rather than see them grow up under foreign rule. The warriors – those who would not surrender and were eventually captured – sang melancholy yet defiant dirges as they marched to the crosses where they were nailed and met their slow deaths. The country, Strabo wrote, was so rich in minerals, metals, and sun that fighting for it was understandable, but the citizens' massacre was blamed instead on the heated, immoderate nature of the Celtic and Iberian blood that ran in these peoples' veins. To the incrementally more tempered Romans, the Spaniards seemed to possess more ardor, sensitivity, and impetuousness than was good for them. And yet, it was this similarity in disposition that, when all was done and the peninsula was firmly under Rome's govern, allowed a close sympathy to form between the two countries and for the people – once invaders, once the conquered – to eventually stand side by side as equals.

For Consuegra, the time of the Romans was a particularly prosperous era. It was perfectly situated – not so far from the sea as to make it inconvenient for travel and trade, and in a favorable part of the country to provide Rome with many of its favorite things. When the Romans took up residence, they moved the center of town down from the hill to give it room to grow, leaving the high ground and its long sloping ridge exclusively for garrison use. They built a wall around enough land – in roughly the same configuration that the town retains today – to allow a sizable community to flourish, then laid out a somewhat orderly grid of streets, the same ones I was rambling through now. The Amarguilla River was crossed with aqueducts and reservoirs and spanned by three substantial stone bridges. Foundations of a thermal bath and a circus are still visible in the eastern part of the town. There would have been at least one temple and a marketplace, but they have disappeared without a trace.

Consuegra thrived for five hundred years before the Visigoths descended upon them and plunged the town into the backwaters, only to be rescued by the Moors, who it seems took an interest in the area merely for its rim of high land. They left behind the castle, a furnace that can be seen in the pottery workshop where the Roman circus used to be, and a healthy saffron trade.

I thought about all of this as I tried to find the farmer's house – how the fierceness of the people the Romans encountered can still be observed in the hard animosity they continue to hold against the Moors – and indeed any foreigners who attempt to settle in the country. (The night before, as I went up to my room through the bar, which was packed with men and families, the children drinking sodas and playing games while their parents talked with friends, I passed behind two men kicking up a sword-rattling ruckus about how the new immigrants coming into the south would bring another "time of the Moors.") And yet, I thought, how transitory and essentially immaterial even the most deeply entrenched influence becomes in the long course of a country's history.

Why else, in an area once brimming with saffron, was I finding it so hard to locate the last saffron farmer in town? It is the simple truth that as Spain has grown away from the shadow of Franco's regime and become one of the more prosperous of the European communities production of saffron has slipped – the work is too demanding, as always too hard. France has once more begun to export a crop, but it is a small amount – a boutique crop at best – while only a small part of the potent and heady Kashmiri harvest manages to pierce through the decades-long combat lines between India and Pakistan. These days the scandal in the saffron world concerns the rising production from Iran – the rebirth of the old Persian crocus fields, cared for and tended by the religious faithful who break their backs in long hours of picking, happy with the earthly pennies they receive for their labor since it is done for the Almighty in Paradise.

In towns such as this one across La Mancha the saffron fields are receding fast, tilled over into vineyards and olive groves, and a way of life – the rituals the flower demands – is disappearing along with it. I walked up and down the Calle Urda thinking that perhaps saffron was already gone from Consuegra. Then I spotted a hand-lettered sandwich-board sign out on the slim sidewalk, painted with a crude crocus blossom, underlined by an arrow pointing to the open doors of a modest house. There, inside, behind the family table, sat a woman in her early sixties; massed on top of the table was a great heap of torn saffron petals, and on a little plate beside the woman's hands was the meager pile of threads she had harvested from them. Her son, who managed the farm, stood behind her selling small bottles of saffron, while her husband stood in front of the table, minding his grandson, who only wanted to throw the blossoms into the air. I leaned against the family's door to watch her work; her fingers flew, picking out a bud, spreading its petals back, plucking the red threads from the center. It was hard to count how many she did, but it would have been close to a hundred or two in the fifteen minutes I stood watching her, though what she gleamed from them added very little to the saucer of threads.

Her husband bid me to come in. “Avanti, avanti,” he smiled, and I drew nearer, my hand reaching to touch the blossoms, fleshy and soft, clinging to my skin.

“May I?” I asked, my English registering as a surprise on the men’s faces while the woman continued to work – her face showing nothing as if she was in a trance.

I mimed picking, and the son cried “Sí, sí!” and portioned off a small bunch of blooms from his mother’s pile. I bent over the table, clumsily pushing back two of the flower’s petals and ripping the threads apart. It was, at once, an intimate and tedious affair – the velvety, sticky petals parted like secret sweaty folds of flesh; the thin stigmas tore, clung stubbornly to the yellow stamens and flower stalk. I blundered on through the pile, getting a little better but not by much, and even after only this small amount I could feel my fingers tingle with numbness. My hands were powdered with amber, and when I raised them to my face I was surprised at how little scent clung to them.

“Gracias,” I murmured as I rubbed the stiffness from my fingers, the yellow tinge working its way under my nails.

The town was rousing itself again from the afternoon slumber and heading through the plaza to a little courtyard where the saffron-picking contest was to be held. The jovial atmosphere that overtook the crowd during the food contest had returned as people pressed through the whitewashed walls into the yard.

Behind a long table covered in white paper sat nine women. The older ones were clad in heavy black sweaters, their black hair primed in neat short coifs exposing beautiful gold earrings dangling from even the eldest contestant’s lobes. The younger ones, on the other hand, were dressed in sporty nylon jackets, light-colored sweaters, their hair dyed red and blond, longer, covering their ears. Near the end of the table was a single man – young and surprisingly corporate looking in a button-down oxford shirt. In front of each contestant was a large handful of blossoms and a white saucer. Television camera crews leaned on the wall behind the table, poised for the action to begin. The audience pressed forward along the edge of the table; others climbed to a balcony running along the far wall and jammed its curved wrought-iron staircase. A teenage girl and a young boy scaled a peach tree planted near the courtyard's water well.

The strange little man I had met earlier in the day stood on a chair with a microphone in his hands and began to speak. The crowd laughed and clapped at what he said. A man in the crowd yelled something out to him that made everyone chuckle, and the two went on with their conversation as if they were the only ones in the courtyard. I overheard an English woman behind me talking to her companion, and I pardoned myself to ask her if she knew who the little man was, if she could tell me what they were saying.

"That's Paco," she said. "He began the festival thirty years ago, and everyone in town complains that he thinks it belongs to him. That is what the man is joking with him about."

But Paco didn't seem to mind the joshing at all. In fact, he seemed to be taking it as his due and grew, if possible, even more magisterial as he went on with his little speech. Then, at some signal, the contestants began their task – silently concentrating, their fingers working without a single wasted motion. Paco jumped down from his pedestal to march slowly behind the table, his hands folded behind his back, watching each of the contestants' progress. The women folded back the petals as if uncovering a gem, the threads plucked as if they were the strings of a harp in a delicate and quick staccato movement; the man tore through the flowers, ripping the petals apart, strewing them every which way about him. When each contestant had gone through their little mound, they stood up behind their chair and Paco surveyed their plate of threads. He stirred his index finger through each dish, checking to see whether much of the yellow part of the flowers' filaments remained attached to the threads, which would make them less pure (and thus less valuable), then fluttered his hand through the petals to see whether any of the threads had been missed. The white paper on the table was streaked with yellow, the petals lay like the crumbled down of ravaged birds. The last to finish was the youngest, a blond woman at the end of the table; there was a tie for first place – between the man and a grandmother. They would be paired tomorrow with contestants from two other nearby towns for the final competition. Everyone clapped and called good wishes to the winners, then streamed from the courtyard, for it was growing late and almost time for the setting of the windmill.

The windmills of Consuegra were built in the German rather than the Dutch style; the sails are attached to a long central pole that allows them to be turned in whatever way the wind is blowing. The four sails were constructed of long tree trunks and branches tied together to form a grid of squares forty feet long, then covered with white cloth to catch the wind. In the tower under the peaked roof of the one working mill was a grinding stone, and each year as part of the festival wheat was ground into flour and distributed among the crowd in small cloth bags. Just a short generation or two ago, Spain was primarily an agricultural nation, and the beauty of the land – and the work it demanded – remains an instinctive part of the culture. The students I had met the day before in the nearby tourist office may have returned to help with the festival, but they would go back to Toledo or Madrid. They would probably find someone in the cities and settle down there with all the conveniences the modern world has to offer. Still, there would be a part of them – as there was a part of every one of the people clambering along the hill to find a seat among the rocks and crevices – wanting to see the country windmills turn, to know how the wind was once seized from the hilltop and used to grind the summer's harvest.

The people gathered close together, jockeying for a good rock to sit upon. As they waited, musicians lined up in the parking lot beside the windmill and were soon joined by a sharply dressed dancing troop. The men wore bolero vests, crisp white shirts, red cummerbunds, and tight black pants. The young women were graced in long red skirts, black tight-fitting jackets, and immense paisley shawls, their heavy black hair pinned tightly back in chignons, their gold earrings glinting in the lowering rays of the sun. One of the men in the troupe I recognized as the young bartender from the hotel, but up here on the hill he looked more handsome, more self-possessed and assured as he took his partner in his arms. The musicians began to play, a woman to chant a plaintive note, then both launched into a rousing song. The dance was formal and yet enormously blithe and seductive; the women slowly swayed their hips from side to side before the men who acknowledged the invitation by straightening their backs, raising their arms with tender strength, and fastening the women with an ardent gaze as they circled around them. Then they turned away from one another, changed partners, repeated the invitation of undulating hips and arching arms – on and on until all the dancers had partnered with one another.

A breeze rubbed across the hump of the hill; the castle's old stones glowed golden in the dying sunlight. A hand jutted from a small window near the windmill's peaked black roof, checking for the wind's direction, and then disappeared inside. The sails were turned slightly toward the face of the hill. Outside two men held steady the sail closest to the ground, while the Dulcinea, her court, the mayor, and Paco arrived. The young girls sprinted up the last of the hill; the two men – especially Paco – had to stop and press their hands against their chests. The court lined up before the dancers, the attendants on either side of the solemn Dulcinea, holding their hands against their slim hips to fan their shawls across their backs. The people on the hillside quieted down when the mayor stepped forward to shout a few words into the hill. I supposed he must have explained the workings of the windmill, giving a lesson in wind management and rotation, for he waved his hands several times to the mill and everyone listened patiently, even somewhat attentively. After him, a priest recited a prayer and sprinkled the mill with holy water. Then a small lever was pushed to unlock the sail's spoke, and everyone near the mill took a big step backward.

Nothing happened.

The wind was full, coming from the right direction, but the sail did not move. The men gave the sail a little push, then a bigger one, shoving it hard, only to see the spoke make one lazy, half-hearted rotation.

The mayor called an old man down from the hill, and he walked around the windmill, checked the sail, went up to the tower, looked out the windows, moved the spoke slightly more toward the hill, and then came back down and outside again. He rotated his arm, and from inside something must have turned, for this time when the men pushed the sail it caught the twilight's breeze and began to spin – first with a creak and then with a smooth musical grind. It was a majestic sight – these four white sails in their pure white tower spinning against the backdrop of the clear evening sky. The musicians launched into another song – a stirring, stamping tune – and the dancers twirled from arm to arm, the women thrown up in the air by one man and caught by another, castanets and heels clicking merrily, the frill of white slips belling out to reveal beautiful legs kicking up against the inking sky.

It seemed that everyone around me was swaying and laughing, children leaping from stone to stone. No one wanted to leave even as the sky swiftly lost its glow and the air turned cold. But gradually, here and there, a retreat began, and I, too, started to pick my way down the hill, tired from the long day, feeling lightheaded with all I had seen and tasted and heard. And as I went, alone but happily so, a man came up to me and presented four crocus blooms he had found growing on the hill beneath the castle. He bowed and told me in decorous, British English, "You will press them in a book, and every time you open it there will be the fragrance of saffron."

And that is what I did. I opened up my hardcover notebook and pressed the fresh blossoms between two blank pages. Today, the purple petals are as sheer as parchment, the stalks golden, the filaments like red veins running beneath the translucent purple skin, and each time I open the book, the pages exhale saffron's impetuous perfume.

III.

I will tell you this truth about travel – one that holds even for such short trips as this one: there is nothing so wonderful as a familiar face. I think of the Phoenicians in their fat boats, gone for months, even years, and wonder how they did it. Or what about Alexander – or more pointedly his men, who without his vision and zeal had only duty to ease their homesick hearts? All those crusaders, those pilgrims, the Venetian merchants, tramping miles through strange lands. Even in the midst of their yearning passions, even in brief passing, did they all not long for one swift glance of a loved one's face?

I was no longer feeling lost – by the third and final day of the festival, I knew my way up and down and around Consuegra. Nor was I homesick, though I would have liked for my husband and sons to have seen all that I had seen, and I thought of them often as I watched couples and families stroll together in the park, laughing and having fun. No, it wasn't anything like that – it was just elementary joy when I saw my sister, Suzanne, enter the hotel that morning, wrapped in a scarlet mohair shawl and pulling a small wheeled valise behind her. She had been at a medical conference in Belgium and did not have to be home for a few more days. It was natural for my sister – the most intrepid of women – to think there was no better way for her to spend her free time than to travel to another country on an overnight train and then a bus, to find me and attend the grand finale of the saffron festival.

The hotel had filled overnight with guests – the dining room the night before had been jammed for the special saffron menu the chef had devised – everything from an appetizer of saffron eggs to dessert of saffron crème brûlée. My sister and I stood hugging and laughing in the middle of the bar crowded with sleepy guests eating their toast and sipping their cups of hot chocolate – all up way too early after the chef's splendid banquet. We must have been talking too loudly, or maybe it was just such a strange sight to see two slightly middle-aged women hooting like school girls, but I caught the elderly proprietor's disapproving eye and felt compelled to tell him, "Mi sister," to which he only shook his head even harder.

We put her bag in my room and off we went to the Plaza Mayor, where a stage had been constructed for the dancing competition. Chairs had been set up before it – including two heavily carved, thronelike chairs upholstered with velvet seats and backs for the Dulcinea and her maid of honor. Long red and saffron-yellow banners hung down the plaza's clock tower, tacked in graceful bunting beneath the square's balconies. Already, an hour before the event was to begin, people had claimed places for themselves and friends. They packed the benches underneath the orange trees. Camera crews from Germany, France, and Japan spooled out power cables and commanded the high ledges and the balcony of the town's museum behind the stage. We felt lucky to grab two spaces on a bench near the stage.

Sue, restless and curious and at heart more of an explorer than I'll ever be, soon went off to take pictures and investigate the nearby buildings. The elegant couple who were seated beside me overheard my sister and me talking, and after she was gone the man leaned over and, in English, introduced himself. His wife spoke only Spanish, but for a few years after completing his studies at the university he had worked in New York and retained fond memories of America.

"I am from Granada," he said, and smiled proudly. "It is the most beautiful of Spain's cities."

"And you came all the way here for the festival?" I asked.

He shrugged his shoulders, dismissing the distance from the southern city to the central plains. "I have not come as far as you," he teased. "But my wife, her family is from here, and she likes to come."

He asked me where else in the country I had been and was surprised at my limited itinerary, that I was going home so soon after seeing only Consuegra, a little bit of Toledo, and as much of Madrid as I could tomorrow. I told him about my interest in saffron, which made him smile even more.

He cocked his head backward toward the castle and curtly commented, "The Arabs. They liked the taste."

"And you?"

He shrugged his shoulders to answer me. "My wife's family used to grow it here, but not anymore."

"Why?"

"Too much work. The young people all want to go to the city and make their money with clean hands."

A little boy suddenly appeared and before I knew it pinned on my blouse a little crocus blossom, its flimsy stem bandaged in a bit of foil.

He was quickly followed by a friend who rattled a can for donations to cancer research. I put a few coins in the can and felt the flower that was already melting in the day's rising heat.

The man beside me adjusted the saffron boutonniere on his wife's jacket, then ran his finger caressingly under her chin. He told me they were meeting friends; they would have lunch later at the hotel, rest there for a while, then go out to see where his wife's family used to live. The land is now part of a big vineyard, and her parents have moved to a town not far away. They live now in a modern house.

"We enjoy our day in the country," he said as they stood up to go meet their friends in the park. "You will enjoy the festival and you must stay to see the dancing."

The couple's place was quickly seized by a magazine photographer and his bag of cameras. The Dulcinea made her entrance with her court. She looked even more regal in a blue brocade gown of Renaissance design, the sleeves and high flaring collar sewn with pearls. The maid of honor – a true beauty – was in rustling black silk that underlined the clear whiteness of her long graceful neck and youthful blush on her checks. Both of them carried long fans, the wood carved into lace, and when they took their seats, the girls snapped them open with a practiced jerk of their wrist and held them to the side of their faces, shielding their eyes from the high sun. I scanned the square for Sue, wondering where she had gotten herself off to. My sister has become like our father. When she is in a new place, she is apt to get lost in talking to whomever she encounters, in finding out what there is to see. I was not surprised that she had been gone for so long, nor was I surprised when I recognized her making her way back to the bench in the company of another woman.

"Look who I found," she announced, as if I would know who the woman was.

"It's so interesting to see you here," the woman laughed. She was an American – but I would have known that even before she spoke, if only by her casual dress, her height, and her open merry face. "I'm Ellen Szita." One of the leading – if not *the* leading – expert on saffron, Ellen, I knew, was someone I would have to talk to, someone whose knowledge and experience was respected by many importers and growers of saffron. Her Web site (www.saffroninfo.com) is nearly encyclopedic; her recipes are just about foolproof.

And yet, I had consciously avoided her. Early on in my research, I had sent her a short note asking for advice but had received no reply and was just as happy. I don't know why. Or perhaps I did – understanding quickly that I would never hold half the knowledge she did and that as much as I came to adore saffron and was intrigued by it, I would never be as consumed by it as she so clearly was. She had changed her life because of the flower – leaving a career as an investigative reporter and foreign correspondent to travel the world watching over saffron fields, lecturing in universities, visiting with importers, keeping tabs on the world's supply. As I stood beside her, I felt my interest to be, at best, steeped from a decidedly less potent strain.

These, however, were my own nuances. I felt her warmth as clear as honey and liked her very much.

"You know I did write back to you," she said without me asking why she didn't. "And essentially I said I couldn't help you that much because we're competing, you see."

"Oh, no," I began to assure her.

But she stilled my protest by asking quickly with her hand cupped around her chin, "When, exactly, was it that you fell in love with saffron?" She reminded me suddenly of one of Henry James's grand, insatiable American women, magnificent in their myopic bluntness.

I could not think of an answer to her question. There hadn't been one particular moment but rather several hits – and though I was enamored of the crocus's smell and taste and how both, like memory, linger to provoke and trouble the senses, I wondered if it really was the spice at all that I loved so much. Maybe it was how such a little flower had incited such things as this festival, her interest, the pleasures of men, the hunger of a race, the fables of storied nations. And that, I sensed, would not be enough for her.

Really, though, I just didn't know, but Sue stepped in and answered for me. "I love saffron bread."

"Oh, if I only knew. I'm making some for these people I stayed with once and you could have come. Of course, the Spanish take saffron for granted. They don't know anything about the culture of it in their country. It's just for the tourist now. " She swept her arms to take in the stage, the Dulcinea on her throne, the throng filling the square.

"All the fields around here used to be purple when the festival began. Now there isn't one. It's dying out – and it will, if the industry doesn't find a way to mechanize the harvesting. And look at what the Iranians are doing! They're flooding the market with cheap prices because the people do it for the love of God!"

Her voice was agitated; she had been trying to get into Iran for years but had been unable to procure a visa. That bothersome situation, however, was quickly glossed over, and somehow the subject became saffron ice cream.

"A fabulous application. Simply fabulous."

"The hotel had a full saffron dinner last night."

"Oh, I'll have to check it out tonight. Are you staying?"

Sue told her we were going to Madrid later in the afternoon.

"Well, look, let's take a picture. I'll give you my address – have you done any research on medicinal applications? We must stay in touch."

We exchanged pictures, exchanged addresses. She gave me a big warm hug and a kiss on the cheek, and then she disappeared, running after a young girl who wore a skirt of the deepest saffron yellow.

"What a hoot," my sister pronounced.

"Where did you find her?"

"I was taking pictures near the stage, and she jumped up right in front of me to get a shot of the saffron queen."

"The Dulcinea?"

Sue waved her hand. "Whatever."

"Why don't I have her passion?"

She shot me a vexing-sister look and then added, "It's a flower. Keep telling yourself that. It's just a flower."

"But not to everyone."

"And that's okay."

With that she pulled me from the bench and closer to the stage, where the finals of the saffron-picking contest were about to be decided and where the musicians from the first dancing troupe were warming up. We stayed in the square long enough to watch the dancing, to admire the handsome men and wish we were one of the young women they were holding in their arms. We left because we were hungry and found a restaurant where we ordered a big meal and a bottle of wine. And for the first time since I had gotten to Consuegra I ate a long, delicious meal – not rushed from loneliness like the ones in the hotel had been (though they had been exquisite, beautiful in every way) – but lingering into the late afternoon, deeply enjoying the flavor of the thin, fresh slices of salmon broiled until it was rimmed by a crisp rosy-brown lip, the bread casserole thickened with smoky sausages and silky potatoes. We ate and drank slowly, talked as sisters do, enjoyed the people around us in their chatting, partying mood, and left more satiated than either of us had been in a while.

We returned to the hotel and retrieved our bags, then walked back into town to the little bus station where just two days before I had gotten off, confused, disoriented, finding myself on a journey more dreamed than planned. We had more glasses of wine in the station's bar before the bus to Madrid pulled up in front, and we joined the other people who had come to Consuegra for the festival and were now leaving, taking seats in the back, away from the little television screen beside the driver that was playing a strange version of "The Pirates of Penzance," starring Olivia Newton John. Sue folded her mohair shawl into a pillow and pressed it against the window to rest her head; I leaned against her shoulder. We slept all the way into Madrid, where for a day and a night we strolled around entirely lost but enchanted by everything.

IV.

The restaurant connected to the Hotel Las Provincias in Consuegra was behind a set of heavily carved doors. I was always too early when I returned at night from the festival for the doors to be open. That first night when I was so very tired and famished after wandering the streets lost for so long – my little repast of tapas having worn off – I leaned against them, listening forlornly through the thick panels to the clicking of glasses and silverware as the waiters set up the tables. I knew the time was too far away for me to stay and see them open for the evening. I tottered to the bar instead, ordered a sherry, and somehow lasted until nine when the doors were magically unlocked and I was allowed to come in. For at least a half an hour, I was the only one sitting there, and then a middle-aged couple came in and sat across the room by the arched windows; by the time I was finished eating the meal that the waitress in pity had helped me to order, the room was full.

It is a constant in Spanish guide books (or, at least, in those for Americans) to give a stern warning about the late hours of dining in Spain, and I will admit that it took some getting used to – especially for someone whose internal clock starts early in the day and peters out soon after sunset. But after that first hard day I fell into step with the rest of the country, and I will tell you this – I would live in Spain happily for the rest of my days on earth if only for the way the country eats. It is so exquisite, and so full of sense, to arise and have nothing more than a bit of toast with milky coffee or hot chocolate, knowing you will stop somewhere around eleven and have a meal that is a little more substantial, perhaps an omelette or a little sandwich made of sausage or ham. At one, it is time for a glass of wine and a tapa or two at a bar, which leads into a hearty lunch with a little more wine, after which you must retire for a small nap. Back at work for a little bit by three – or even four (for what's the hurry when twilight lingers so complaisantly?) – until the clock strikes six and it's off to find a comfortable seat at another bar for another glass of wine or a sherry, and some more tapas and talk with friends to see how the day has gone so far or to plan the evening. By the next time you look up, it's after ten o'clock and you're a little more than famished, despite the little plates of tapas that have piled up around your glass. And so you all go off down the street to a little restaurant that makes the very best cod stew, and after that, though it may be past midnight, the lights are still on in the Plaza Mayor, and music flows from an open doorway to entice you away from bed.

In other words, the day revolves around eating, a constant roundelay of small meals and glasses of wine, just enough to keep the stomach slightly full and the spirit happy. More propitious, though, are the pauses the regime builds into the day, providing time enough to enjoy what is actually put before you, time to collect thoughts, to ponder the day, and to engage in conversation. Even within that forced mute, powerless state of being the *other,* I found in sharing a dish, a glass of wine, the most elementary of communal languages, which makes the simplest meal richer than what the finest chef could ever supply.

That was why I was quite happy with all of this – and extremely happy the times I dined in the hotel's restaurant. It was a very pretty room, with brick arches and whitewashed walls decorated with historical photographs of the town. The servers – a young woman with a pierced nose and many earrings and two men of equal youth and primary-colored hair to show their rebellion – were good at their job, kind and sweet-natured, swift and unobtrusive.

Best of all was the chef – the young man who had helped with my reservation. He could not have been older than thirty, and I suspect he was much younger than that. The hotel owner told me he was a student from France who had come to Spain, and especially this little outpost, to prove his kitchen mettle and perhaps make a few contacts at the saffron festival. When I saw him in the courtyard relaxing with the kitchen staff at their afternoon meal, all of them eating from a great pot in the middle of the table, with loafs of broken bread and bottles of wine between their plates, he seemed to be so very much in command, more than his age would seem to allow. And indeed it was his skill, the very masterfulness of the dishes he made each night for the restaurant, that proved his worth.

For the saffron festival, the chef made a menu for Saturday night that was naturally composed of dishes with saffron in them: white fish in saffron, the traditional bread and sausage casserole I had had earlier in the day, an old country recipe made with chicken livers and eggs, a rabbit dish and a shrimp one, and finally the crème brûlée that I have previously mentioned.

There was also this offering – a very old recipe that I noticed a young family ordering. The parents were both very stylish and beautiful, even glamorous. The woman wore a white silk blouse and a soft tight skirt made of calfskin. The husband had on a gray, intricately woven vest over a fine white cotton shirt and black pants. Their daughter of eight or nine, long hair in a thick braid and carrying a plastic purse with tufts of fur on it and stuffed full with little furry animals, pins, barrettes, and games, was in jeans and a pullover. She appeared like any other child but with an edge of sophistication that matched her parents' and was allowed to order for herself a glass of sweet sherry heavily diluted with water.

For their dinner, they ordered chicken al andalus. It came in a large shallow copper casserole, and they all dug into it with robust delight. There are, in this one old dish, all the flavors the Moors left behind in the country, and for that reason alone, the taste is subtle, yet intense, thick with nuance and mystery.

Chicken al Andalus

6 tablespoons olive oil
1 thick slice of country bread, cut into cubes
2 garlic cloves, crushed and minced
3 pounds chicken pieces
1 large sweet onion, finely chopped
2½ cups water
½ teaspoon ground cinnamon
½ teaspoon ground cloves
3 tablespoons almond, roughly chopped
a small pinch of saffron (if you're counting, about 30 threads)
½ teaspoon cumin seeds
2 hard-boiled egg yolks
salt and pepper to taste

Heat the oil in a flameproof casserole and sauté the bread cubes and garlic until they all turn a light shade of brown. Remove with a slotted spoon and reserve.

Lower the heat on the oil and sauté the chicken pieces until golden. Remove with a slotted spoon and set aside. In the same oil, fry the onions until soft. Lay the chicken over the onions; add the bread cubes and garlic, sprinkling them over the top of the chicken. Pour in the water; squeeze the lemon over the chicken, add the cinnamon and cloves. Cover and cook on a low heat for one hour.

Meanwhile, toast the almonds in a little olive oil until slightly brown. Place the almonds in a mortar with the saffron and pound them both together. Add the cumin seeds and pound until fine. Add the egg yolks and pound to a thick paste. Add a little bit of the cooking liquid from the casserole to moisten the paste. Set aside for at least twenty minutes to allow the saffron to brew.

When the chicken is almost done, add the saffron-almond paste, stirring it in until it dissolves fully. Add salt and pepper to taste. You can serve this dish with plain rice. It also goes very nicely with small new potatoes, boiled and plainly dressed with sweet butter. Serves 6.

For my dinner I chose lamb stew, though I thought about the liver and eggs simply because I always think I should taste something I would never make for myself. But after such a long day, the lamb seemed kinder to me. Again, it is an old dish. I have seen it referred to in cookbooks as a shepherd's meal, commonly cooked outdoors over an open flame, which would give it a little more of a smoky edge than the elegant version I had at the restaurant. I have also heard – and read – of it being made with goat.

Caldereta Cordero

⅔ cup olive oil
4 cloves garlic, peeled
2 bay leaves
1 tablespoon paprika
1 bottle (750 ml) dry white wine
3 pounds lamb, cubed
½ pound lamb liver, in one piece
a pinch of saffron (about 30 threads)
salt and freshly ground pepper
to taste

Heat the oil in a medium-sized stockpot and sauté the garlic cloves until brown. Add the lamb pieces and the liver and sauté until brown. Remove the liver and set aside. To the meat, add the bay leaves and paprika and stir. Add the wine – enough to cover the meat. Lower the heat. Cover and let cook undisturbed until the meat is tender, about 45 minutes to an hour.

About a half hour before the meat is done, spoon a little of the hot cooking liquid into a bowl (about 2 tablespoons). Stir the saffron into the liquid and let it steep. Add the saffron to the meat, stir, and remove from heat. Let the casserole rest, covered, for about ten minutes.

Before serving, check seasonings. Add salt and pepper to taste and serve. Serves 6.

I have not been able to find a precise recipe for the bread crumb and sausage dish cooked at the contest, but I have found the chicken dish in a little handout I got from the tourist office in Consuegra, and it tastes just like what I remember – a little sour, a little sweet. You don't need to scrounge around for an old chicken – I think the idea here is to find the most flavorful bird. You want the sweet taste of the flesh to play off the other ingredients.

Gallina Pepitoria

2 slices of country-style bread
2 tablespoons olive oil
2 tablespoons red wine vinegar
1 medium onion, peeled and quartered
1 whole head of garlic, the cloves peeled
2 chicken livers
1 chicken, 5 to 6 pounds, skinned and cut into serving pieces
1 handful (about ⅔ cup) almonds
1 tablespoon whole black peppercorns
a large pinch of saffron (about 45–50 threads)
about ½ cup fresh parsley leaves
salt to taste

In a large skillet, fry the bread slices in olive oil until golden. Remove with a slotted spoon to a plate and drizzle the vinegar over them. Reserve. In the same oil, sauté the onion, garlic cloves, and chicken livers until the onion and cloves are golden and the liver is cooked through. Remove them with a slotted spoon and drain well on a paper towel.

Puree the bread slices, onion, garlic, and chicken livers in the bowl of a food processor fitted with a metal blade, stopping once or twice to scrape down the sides of the bowl. Reserve. In the same olive oil, over medium heat, brown the chicken pieces (you may have to add a little more oil, but not too much). When all of the chicken has been browned, add the pureed bread mixture and stir together, cooking for about five minutes.

Meanwhile, using a mortar and pestle, pound the almonds into small pieces and add to the chicken; then pound the peppercorns with the saffron and parsley. (You can do this in batches if your mortar isn't big enough – just empty each batch into a bowl.) Add about a tablespoon of hot water to the peppercorn-saffron mixture and let steep for 15 to 20 minutes. (For a slightly more astringent flavor, you can steep the mixture in a tablespoon of wine vinegar instead of hot water.)

Add the peppercorn-saffron mixture to the chicken, stirring well. Cover the skillet, lower the heat, and cook until the chicken is cooked through and tender. Before serving, taste and add salt, if desired. Serves 6 to 8.

I did not have the following dish in Consuegra – I tasted it in Madrid, at a little bar that Sue and I wandered into very late. It was crowded with tourists, and it took some time to push toward the bar where enormous platters of food were laid out – vinegary tiny anchovies, broiled sardines, chickpeas in a thick tomato sauce, sausages of every kind. The bar was filled with young Americans on their year abroad – blasé young women trying to look sophisticated as they perched on the edge of the wooden stools, in one hand a cigarette, in the other a glass of wine (usually white, to keep their figures trim), their fashionably small purses hanging from the crook of their arm. They mewed – audibly, like tired, petulant kittens – when we inched by them, excusing ourselves in English ("Oh, God," my sister mimicked, "our *mothers*"). The young men seemed to be enjoying themselves more, if only because they were free from keeping up appearances and the pressure of acquiring the veneer of a European experience.

We discovered two empty seats at the bar and soon fell into conversation with the boys beside us. One was eager to get back home and go to graduate school, eager, now that he had been away a year, to begin his life. The other was earnestly on the prowl and, after several carafes of wine, made the startling proclamation that he was extremely fertile as he looked about the room at all the available women. We asked whether, perhaps, he meant *virile*. And he sheepishly smiled in an endearing way and replied, "Oh, yeah, right." We laughed away his mistake and insisted on buying them both more wine, then toasted the evening and wished them success before we shoved off to our opposite pursuits – the boys to a table full of girls across the room and Sue and I to the food at the other end of the bar.

What we decided to try was the one dish that only the Spaniards seemed to be choosing, which turned out to be marinated rabbit – *conejo en escabeche* – a dish of medieval origins that is served cold or at room temperature and is just the right thing to have, along with several glasses of red wine, to be sent happily off to bed. It makes it a handy dish to have around during the holidays. You don't want a great deal of it at one sitting, so it will satisfy a small crowd, and it keeps fairly well in the refrigerator for a week.

Conejo en Escabeche

4 pounds rabbit, chopped into small serving pieces
salt to taste
¾ cup olive oil
1 whole head of garlic
2 bay leaves
1 tablespoon finely chopped parsley
1 tablespoon whole black peppercorns
4 cloves
peel from three medium-sized oranges, cut into slivers
peel from four lemons, cut into slivers
¾ cup dry red wine
2¼ cups water
1 large pinch saffron (about 40–45 threads)

Sprinkle the rabbit pieces with the salt. In a large sauté pan, heat the oil and sauté the rabbit pieces until brown. Add all the other ingredients (including the saffron threads, but make sure they are stirred into the liquid and are not left on the meat), burying the head of garlic in the middle of the meat. Cover the pan, lower the heat to simmer, and cook for about 1 to 1½ hours (adding more wine if necessary), or until the meat is tender.

Remove from heat. Let the meat cool in the pan with its juices; pack the meat and the juices – with the garlic bowl buried at the center – into an earthenware bowl or crock and refrigerate for about 48 hours before serving.

To serve: The way we saw people eating this dish in the bar was to take a couple of garlic cloves – the bulb will easily break apart and be soft after all the cooking – and press your fork against the cloves to release them from their papery skin. Smear the softened clove onto a piece of meat before eating. Some people broke off pieces of bread and pushed the meat and garlic into the bread and then dipped it into the sauce. That's what I did because it gathered so much of the flavors together and brought them in somewhat of a respectable manner to my lips. Do not expect this to be anything but a succulent rough dish. There is nothing refined about it. If you understand that, and serve it to friends with many glasses of good bold red wine and ample bread, you will understand and appreciate its delectable sophistication. Serves at least 6.

The Saffron Fields of Brooklyn

Such frail red threads,
odd how they bleed so yellow, so contrary
to what a purple flower's genitals
should look like.

CRAIG ARNOLD, "SAFFRON"

I.

I have thought about the question Ellen Szita posed to me in Consuegra a thousand times over. When, exactly, did I fall in love with saffron? Was it truly in that cold kitchen so many nights ago when Michael drew me from the bedroom with the scent of it boring through hard shells to pierce the soft flesh of clams and lobsters, all my feverish fervor roused by it instead of by the man offering himself to me? Or was that just the flowering, after a bed had been prepared years before – not on those family drives through Lancaster when my parents were young and we were happy, but in the confines of a small humid kitchen, in the company of a woman who swayed from stove to counter, from cupboard to sink, not exactly knowing, as my mother did, what she was doing but, in her bare feet and with a stemmed martini glass at her side, imparting to me (who was no more than five years old, roosting on a stool beside her) one of her most heartfelt secrets: if you add enough saffron to a pan of bubbling rice, the evening's party will be a fabulous success?

This is what I thought about in June as I planted five hundred small corms in a narrow strip of dirt beneath the basketball hoop behind the garden fence and in an even smaller patch across the street in the middle of a vacant lot. No one should do that much work if not for love, but what sustained me had less to do with saffron's flavor or even its potency, for if these were the essence at the heart of this bothersome question then, no, I would not have worked through those hot days as diligently as I did for the few threads I knew I would be lucky to harvest if the corms bloomed. What claimed me more was the promise of a purple sweep of color under an autumn sky and this memory of Mrs. Coogan calling me to celebrate, as I would want to celebrate, after all was said and done.

Every child has a master teacher beyond her parents, and Mrs. Coogan was mine. The Coogans lived at the top of our street in Philadelphia in a row house just like ours. But they were different from everyone else in our working-class neighborhood because the parents had not only gone to college but they were both writers of some note. When they moved into the neighborhood, they had two children – a boy, Kevin, and a girl, Nell, who became my best friend. Forty years after they met, my mom would still tell with astonishment the story of Mrs. Coogan's audacious first visit to our house. One afternoon, the doorbell rang, and my mom opened the front door to find standing on our stoop a tall, large-boned, handsome woman with the brightest shade of fuchsia lipstick freshly painted on her generous mouth.

"My name is Jean Maria," Mrs. Coogan announced in her breathlessly girlish voice. "I just moved in up the street and I've heard your husband is a college graduate and that you're a great reader. Well, we are too, and I'd like us to be friends because I really don't understand how I'm going to live here if I don't find someone to talk to."

It was clear to my mom that the woman was upset and in need of help, so even though she was still trying to sort out what Mrs. Coogan had said, she invited her inside, and within an hour, over coffee and one of my mom's pies, the women became fast friends.

According to my mom, Mrs. Coogan's main misfortune in life was in having had an overly protective and doting mother, who instead of teaching her to cook and keep house had sent her off to a fancy convent school and university. The women in the neighborhood simply could not figure out what Mrs. Coogan did all day while her tables gathered dust and her children were selling potato chip sandwiches to the rest of the kids on the block. Surely this was a woman (and therefore a family) headed for trouble, and many took the precaution of steering clear of the entire clan.

But my mom understood Mrs. Coogan, for although my mom was a remarkable cook and a meticulous cleaner, she was also a great reader who was thrilled to find someone she could talk to, especially in those afternoon hours of a young housewife's day when there was nothing more to clean, the children were down for naps, and dinner and her husband's return from the world were still hours away. The two women fell into the habit of spending this time together, each in her way helping the other to navigate through the tangled straits of ordinary life.

In particular, Mrs. Coogan relied on my mom to show her how to cook. She seemed not to have any natural talents in this regard and was, in fact, capable of being completely flummoxed by the intricacies of even the simplest recipes. The neighborhood grew accustomed to seeing her fly down the hill from her house into ours with a cookbook flapping in her hands, all in a state, needing my mom to translate some elementary cooking instruction. She did this most often when she was about to give a party, because she always wanted something gala and extravagant for her guests, and in the days before she could afford a caterer that meant she had to make it herself, usually with my mom's timely intervention.

The Coogans gave a lot of parties. It doesn't seem to me now that Mr. Coogan was a very social man, because he was always in his study writing, but they had a wide circle of friends, and Mrs. Coogan liked the excitement a party brought to the house. She often heightened the excitement by taking to her bed in the days or hours before the party, resisting the cleaning and shopping a party requires. At the very last possible moment, when everyone else had given up hope, Mrs. Coogan would burst from her room and, in a whirl of activity, somehow got done what needed to be done. What she did love was the party itself – the hosting and the greeting, talking and laughing with her guests, drinking and eating and talking some more until well into the night. Their house appeared always to be in a state of animation, with a party being planned or just hours away. The only time all seemed quiet was in the suspended hush of the "day after," when our parents remained in bed and Nell and I would make a game of finding all the small silver bowls of nuts and mints and half-empty glasses hidden about the messy rooms.

"Patty, sweet puss, do you think you can help me with this?" she asked one day when my mom wasn't around. Mrs. Coogan had called me in from the yard where I had been playing with Nell. She helped me up on a stool beside the counter to show me a magazine spread of something I had never seen before – a bowl of golden rice.

"We need to make enough for twenty and the recipe is only for six. So I guess four times everything?"

That sounded good to me, and when she put four green peppers down in front of me and asked me to cut them up, I thought that was pretty good, too. I was not allowed to touch knives at home, but her faith in me was complete, and I boldly took the small paring knife from her hand and began to cut the strips of pepper as carefully as I could. Mrs. Coogan kicked off her shoes and disappeared into the living room; when she came back, she was carrying a martini glass and rowdy music suddenly exploded around us. I cut the peppers. She chopped onions. Nell came in from the yard, asked if she could cut something too but quickly grew bored with all the peppers. Her eyes watered from the onions, and she soon wandered off. Mrs. Coogan took a sip from her glass and began to sway her hips to the music as she sautéed the vegetables together in an enormous black skillet. She didn't seem to mind, or even see, the bits and pieces of onions and peppers that splattered to the floor, for she kept up a lively patter between us and continued to stir the vegetables in the pan. I can't imagine what it was we talked about, but it was thrilling to feel all her interest zeroed in on me, on whatever it was I was telling her. Best of all, after I opened some cans of tomatoes for her, she whisked me down from the stool and, to a particularly raucous tune, swung me across the floor in a lively, all-the-way-down-to-the-ground-and up-again manic version of a twisting jitterbug.

When we had finished dancing, I climbed back on the stool and she dug around in the cupboard until she found a glass tube full of red threads. She pulled the cork from it and put it under my nose.

"Smell," she commanded. I took a big whiff and reeled my head away from the cold acerbic scent that curled from the vial.

"Now look at this." Mrs. Coogan shook the tangled ball of threads out into her palm, dropped a few into a coffee cup, added a little hot water, then stirred the mixture with her finger. The threads seem to swell and burst open, bleeding yellow across the water like the sun setting behind a still lake. The scent rose lightly off the water, almost sweet but as citric as a lemon. Before she poured the threads into the rice, she told me to dip a fingertip into the water and place a drop of the liquid on my tongue.

"Isn't that something?" She laughed at the frown I made as the taste melted like warm metal across my mouth. As she stirred the water into the rice, the white kernels began to turn yellow – first a pale creamy shade and then a darker, almost orange hue.

When I got home later and excitedly told my mom about what Mrs. Coogan and I had cooked, my mom appeared horrified. I thought it was about the knife or the funny stuff Mrs. Coogan let me taste. But a few minutes later when my dad arrived home from work, I heard her talking about the single bowl of rice that would feed the party that night. My dad opened a bottle of beer and said something about making a snack. My mom shrugged her shoulders and, casting a suspicious eye toward me, hoped out loud that the party wouldn't be spoiled.

I lay in bed that night with my sister curled asleep against my back and listened to the music from the Coogans' house flutter down the hill. I wondered whether Nell had been allowed to stay up, as she sometimes was. Maybe she had put on a party dress and was twisting with her mom in the living room. I thought about slipping past the babysitter downstairs and skipping up the hill, through the back door, filling my belly with perfumed rice, and dancing, dancing. When I awoke again, it was pitched dark and the music had stopped. I heard my parents on the stairs, their voices slippery, excited, and I knew the party had been a success. I was sure the rice Mrs. Coogan and I had made had contributed at least a little to the merriment. As the door closed softly behind my parents, as the night once more quieted, I lay awake hankering to cook up a party again and tickled by the strange taste still lightly simmering on my tongue.

II.

When I ordered the saffron corms last winter from a small nursery in Virginia, all I considered was the promise of a last burst of color that would give the garden a final burnish before winter crept across the beds. But after they arrived, I realized I really didn't have any place to put them. Most city gardens are small – mine is smaller still, crowded with old rose bushes I inherited from the previous owners and my own haphazard, overgrown arrangement of perennials and fruit trees. But there was a tiny triangle of vacant dirt across the street next to a house that had been up for sale for years, which didn't seem likely to be sold anytime soon. If that wasn't enough, I thought about the ground beneath the kids' basketball hoop behind the garden fence out in the communal driveway. Surely Theophrastus would approve of both sites, since the crocuses would more than likely receive resounding tramples in either location. What is more, as Richard Hakluyt admonished his Essex neighbors to consider, both plots faced south, were well sheltered from damning winds, and were the glad recipients of strong sunlight.

Toward the middle of May, I began to wander casually across the street to clear a space toward the middle of the lot where the flowers would be well hidden. I bagged up weeds along with beer bottles, soda cans, cigarette butts, cigar bands from kids making blunts, those minuscule zip-top plastic bags that drugs are sold in these days, a couple of condoms, assorted debris left over from school lunches, a forgotten doll, handfuls of discarded AA batteries, and pages from what looked to be a fairly interesting mail-order catalog for adult videos. At the same time, I outlined a field in old bricks and stones underneath the basketball hoop, then broke through the hard dirt (and a portion of concrete driveway) and mixed in bags and bags of equal parts loam, manure, peat, and sand. I finished with both sites the day before the box of corms arrived, and early the next morning I began to plant them in neat rows six inches deep. It took me three days to plant all the corms; by the end there was reason to fear my back would never straighten again.

But oh, what a lovely, tidy vision my two fields made! Neither, it is true, presented as glorious a sight as the landscape of saffron's foreign homes, but in the confines of their urban borders they were still marvels to behold. And the Brooklyn weather cooperated by remaining dry – for long stretches even approaching hotly arid. Now and then I hauled a watering can over to the lot and hosed the bed under the hoop. For a long time both beds appeared like barren stretches of dirt, a favorite spot for lulling cats and kids hard up for a sand box.

Then, suddenly, the house next door to the lot sold. When the new neighbors quickly moved in, I meant to be friendly and introduce myself, then tell them about the adjoining saffron field, but somehow, between shyness and work, the days got away from me and I never did. A month later, I came out to find that the new neighbors had succeeded in buying the little lot and were busy turning up the dirt to plant grass seed. Like fields across the world, my saffron plot was lost to shortsightedness and progress. I turned back inside the house, yelling at my lax foolishness but hoping that some of the corms would survive. All my attention then fell to the field beneath the basketball hoop, and near the end of August the first shoots appeared. There could have been some across the street as well, but the lot had been transformed into a beautiful lawn, and on top of the spot where I had planted the corms now stood a tiny playhouse for the new neighbors' daughter to play in.

Beneath the hoop, though, was a remarkable sight. The force of being born thrusts a little bit of the corm along with the tightly wrapped blossom arrowheads to the surface. Leaves emerge more slowly and look more like chives or thin blades of grass than anything belonging to a flower. One day, one of my neighbors came up to me while I was watering the field and told me she'd be willing to give me some chemical she had that would rid the ground of what appeared to her like pesky onion grass. I politely declined her offer and kept a closer watch on my crop.

By the middle of September, however, the dirt was covered with lavender spears wearing thick green ruffles, and I began to worry about the invading autumn chill. The Pennsylvania Dutch struggled against the cold that descends early during the northern nights, and this field was even farther north than theirs had been. I thought about ways to keep the plants warm but was saved from having to do anything by the sudden rise of an Indian summer. While the days grew shorter, they remained hot and blessedly dried. Each day the flowers emerged just a little more, while the rest of my garden slowly dwindled. The roses put out their last blooms; the spent tomato vines turned pale and proceeded to wither on their scaffolding. The trees turned red and yellow. The fallen leaves washed in waves across the narrow saffron plain. A few times I came out to find squirrels furtively digging and then racing away into the trees with the flower stalks protruding from their stuffed mouths. I have read that rats, rabbits, and deer also pounce on what must be a succulent gourmet treat for them. I'm pretty sure my field was safe from rabbits and deer, but squirrels were not the only diners to discover this rare bounty. For both the squirrels and the other midnight raider, I blanketed the flowers with cayenne pepper and did not seem to be bothered by either again.

Then, one morning, without any advance warning, the blossoms began to unfurl – the ground was awash in a lavender vapor. The sun was barely up; the air was sugary with frost. I gave a yelp and ran for an old plant saucer, and then I began to pick. Neighbors leaving for work stopped at the sight of my robe hiked up around my thighs as I straddled the rows, bending from the waist, actually tearing out flowers. My children sneaked off to school, too embarrassed to come say good-bye to me; before he left for work my husband, Chris, stood watching me for a while with a crooked little smile on his lips. He may have kissed me good-bye. I don't remember now, and I probably didn't take note of it then, so desperate was I to gather in the harvest.

The saucer was piled high with soft petals when I finally returned to the house. I needed a cup of tea and something to eat; my fingers were wet with dew, sticky with pollen, aching with the morning's chill and toil. The small of my back screamed. My thighs pulled taut. Still, there was work to be done, and I hurriedly dressed and then settled in at the dining room table.

The blossoms at the bottom of the pile were already starting to crumble. I spread the flowers across the dining room table, chased the cats away from their investigation, and tried to remember how the women of Consuegra picked the threads, the way that must have been handed down through the ages from the time of the busy Sumerians. What looks at first blush to be elementary actually takes a bit of practice to get right. The stigmas are delicate and will break in half if you yank too hard. Or the yellow stamen will pull off with the threads and dilute the threads' power when they dry. After you have gone through only a few blossoms, your fingers become moist with pollen and torn petals stick to your skin; fingertips grow numb, and eyes begin to burn under the strain of distinguishing stigma from stamen. It is stupefying, tedious work, made even harder for how you have to harden your heart to rip out the core of such a delicate flower.

I worked until early afternoon and, by the last blossom, had covered a saucer with threads. It seemed like a lot and I was pleased, eager to dry them and see what I had really reaped. There are several ways to dry the threads: the common way is in a very low oven (about 100 degrees Fahrenheit). But you have to trust your oven and keep a careful watch at the door because the threads will burn in the space of a heartbeat. Another way – tried and true – is to dry them on a windowsill on a piece of screen. I considered this method for a while but then added up the number of curious, pesky pets and kids there are in the house and came up with another technique: I laid the threads out on a small pie tin and placed it on top of the warm radiator in the living room. I checked on them every fifteen minutes. The tin became dewy with sweat, and I shifted the threads to a drier spot. An hour or two later, the long threads were beginning to shrink. I shook the tin around some more, stirred the threads with my finger to spread them out, and then kept the pan on the gentle heat a little while longer because even one slightly damp thread will rot a whole jar. By early evening, the first batch was done, and a light musky scent strayed through the house. But all that had once covered a saucer now barely filled a teaspoon.

The harvest went on for several more days. Some flowers had survived in the neighbors' lot, and when no one was looking I picked a couple but felt better about watching their daughter stoop over the mysterious blossoms in wonder and gingerly pick one to give to her mom. Anyway, there seemed to be plenty popping up beneath the hoop. Each corm will put out three flowers, each bloom opening one at a time. Some mornings there were only a few to gather; other times there was a slew. My fingers turned an increasingly darker shade of yellow until they were almost orange; my palms became daffodil-hued. At night the scent rubbed off on the pillow and sheets and seem to burrow into our dreams. By the weekend, I called in my friend Maria to help with the last batch. Many Spanish painters, particularly through the nineteenth century, have used the saffron harvest as a subject, perhaps because it allows for the pleasing depiction of robust peasants bending over fields bathed in morning light or for an alluring gathering of beautiful young women sitting back in rustic wooden chairs, their colorful skirts spread across their laps, their slipping shawls revealing bare burnished shoulders. Even the clumsiest artist cannot help but capture both the sense of companionship and the essential concentration at the heart of the harvest. Maria and I were nowhere near as picturesque, but as we labored through the rest of the afternoon, fueling ourselves first with tea, then moving on to wine, a little gossip, and much laughter, it slowly dawned on me what must have been true through all the thousands of years of saffron's history: you cannot endure saffron's brutal harvest unless you firmly believe in its power and hold it dear. You must cherish the fact that at the heart of this flower lies a force strong enough to bless you, cure you, feed you, make you more beautiful, more rich, more powerful. Without this fervent kind of faith, when no tools – ancient or modern – have been found to alleviate the hard physical labor – saffron would have surely died out long ago.

When the work was finally over and Maria had gone home with her own small measure of threads, I stood in the kitchen staring at the harvest – perhaps no more than a few tablespoons.

"Now what?" Chris asked as I poured the threads into a jar.

"A party," I answered and took my sore bones to bed.

III.

I wanted the party to be near the field, and I wanted to cook the way they did in Consuegra's park. Our ordinary metal grill, wobbly and grimy after the long summer, would not do, so I built a fire pit from river stones, cinder blocks, and old broken bricks and filled its center with a thick bed of oak and apple branches and chips from London plane and black walnut trees I had gathered from the embankment above the expressway. Although it was November and the skies above

Brooklyn were bruised by a chilly fog, our friends sat happily bundled in sweaters and shawls at a nearby table, drinking beer and a thick red wine while the fire sputtered to life. Richard, the wonderfully grumbling chef who lives up the street, knelt beside me to pin a big thrashing lobster against the ground, plunged a knife behind its head, and in one graceful stroke slit the body down the middle. When the fire became steady, we laid a grill over the stones and Richard set down a large sauté pan, poured in olive oil and then a handful of Spanish saffron. The oil flushed the iridescent tint of a pomegranate seed. Hunkered down beside the fire and quickly turning the lobster in the oil from its belly to its back, Richard said the secret to the dish was in both the freshness of the shellfish (as he described it, making sure to chose the one climbing up the fishmonger's tank on the backs of the lazier specimens), and in cooking the lobster with the shell side down in the saffron oil so that the flavor slowly impregnates, rather than saturates, the flesh.

The first person I had thought to invite to the party was Spencer, because he had called late one night to tell me he had grown famished reading a poem written by Craig Arnold called "Saffron." A few days later, the poem on a torn piece of newsprint arrived from him in the mail. I hung it over my desk and, through all these many months, I found myself turning toward it, whispering the stanzas as if they would lead me to understand what it was about saffron that beguiled me so. The lines I repeated the most are these:

There can't be that much saffron in the world
– as if to think it passed through my hands twice
would make it all appear less of a waste,

that wild, endlessly nuanced fugue of flavor,
so much variety, so much to spend.

Spencer sat at the table now, with his wife, Jane, who was deep in intimate conversation with Maria about a man Maria had just lost. Richard's wife, Carol, went about lighting candles as night moved quickly across the garden and then helped to serve the lobster, cracking it into small servings for each of us and pooling a little of the sauce over the meat. There were other things on the table as well – a dish of firm, plump black olives; a small bowl of anchovies mashed with capers and smoked red peppers; wee briny shrimp soaked in garlic, lemon, and wine; a basket piled high with a dense, crusty bread. It pleased me to hear my friends' laughter behind me as I knelt by the fire and laid a few more branches across the smoldering embers; I then began to sauté in my mother's stockpot a heap of chopped garlic. When the pearl white slivers turned dusky, I layered inside the pot pieces of chicken, sweet sausage, the last of the tomatoes from the garden, and a bottle of white wine in which I had steeped most of my saffron crop. I shifted the pot around the flames to find the hottest spot, brought the liquid to a boil, then moved it to a simmering place to brew.

More beers were opened, and more wine was poured. We pulled the silky flesh from the lobster shell and dipped pieces of bread into the saffron juice. When the chicken was ready, I portioned it out and took my place across from Chris. As friends are wont to do when gathered around a cordial table, our manners soon slipped away to pick at bones, each of us succumbing to the innocent hunt for every dainty scrap of burned skin and toasted slivers of garlic. Only after we were sure nothing remained in the pot, would we consider the waiting strong coffee and a warm apple tart.

The candles burned low and we stirred the glowing embers in the fire bed, moving our chairs close to its steady warmth and sipping at a strange syrupy liqueur Richard had brought us from his restaurant. We sat like this for a very long time, lulled by what we had eaten and what we had drunk, yes, but also, I think, because the cool night made us mindful of the season – of time – slipping away and we were reluctant to let it go without marking its passage. Here, at last, in the peace around the fire, in the companionship of friends, I found the answer to the question that had haunted me since Consuegra, that echoed through all these ancient stories, myths, and legends, that informs this beautiful poem and lies at the heart of Mrs. Coogan's invaluable lesson. It is, at last, what this tiny flower has always embodied and through the ages shared with the world – that so little is needed to turn life into a sumptuous feast.

And so we stood, faced the sable darkness covering the slumbering saffron field, and raised our glasses in thanks and praise for this, the most blessed reward of its golden harvest.

A Short Guide to Buying and Using Saffron

Buying Saffron

There is no getting around the fact that buying saffron is a lot like buying illicit drugs. The concerns for purity and potency are the same, as are where it is grown and how it is processed. You may also have to go through some trial and error before you find a reliable, and steady, supplier.

Saffron is not so widely used in America in part because of culture, but also because it *is* such a strange substance. Saffron, unlike any other spice, can't just be used straight from the jar. With each new batch you buy you may want to check its potency to gauge how much you should use in recipes. Potency changes from crop to crop and year to year, and there is absolutely nothing so off-putting as too much saffron in a dish. That said, there is also no other spice that will add so much flavor and beauty to a recipe, and it is well worth a little work to learn to use it well.

The first thing to do is to buy good saffron. It is a pretty safe bet that you won't find it among the spice jars at your local supermarket. If you do, beware – it may have been sitting on the shelf for a very long time under less-than-ideal conditions. Even if it hasn't, the price will be ridiculous for what will probably be very few threads. Your best bet is to seek out specialty food stores or ethnic markets in your area. Indian and Arab neighborhoods are sure to have stores that sell saffron, and it will be fresher and less expensive than anywhere else. The Internet is another good source, and I have listed a couple of trustworthy sites below.

A handful of countries are currently exporting saffron, and although all of it comes from the saffron crocus, growing conditions and production values fluctuate so greatly that the taste varies from country to country. Spanish saffron is generally a little more mellow than saffron from Italy. Kashmiri saffron is intense, but the best-quality product is protected by an Indian export ban (and a never-ending war) and is rarely shipped outside the country; Macedonian Greek saffron will knock your socks off; Persian – if you can find it – smells and tastes like the mother lode. Pennsylvania Dutch saffron is similar to Persian in intensity, but so little of it is produced that it is nearly impossible to find. In recent years, what I would call boutique crops have come on the market – some from the old fields of France, Switzerland, and England. Gentleman farmers around the United States have been taken with the fancy idea of planting their own saffron fields. I have lately heard of some pretty good saffron coming out of New Zealand, too. I wouldn't shun any of these so long as they're pure.

Here's where the difficulty lies though. Things haven't changed much since the Middle Ages. Saffron is still somewhat expensive, and as a result a lot of adulteration still goes on (though I haven't heard of anyone being drawn and quartered for it today). It's very hard to look at saffron in a box and know whether or not it's pure. Certainly the threads should be red with very little yellow stamen mixed in with the lot. Sometimes – but not often enough – the package carries the International Standard Organization (ISO) rating for the crop's coloring strength (which is the best way to figure the threads potency). The ISO has set the minimum world requirement at 190 degrees. Many saffron experts suggest you ask the merchant what the ISO rating is for the saffron they sell. This is sort of a two-prong trick question because in one stroke – as the experts' thinking goes – you'll be able to find a reliable saffron merchant and the quality of his or her stock. I haven't met too many merchants, but the ones I have (both reputable and not) didn't know what I was talking about. My recommendation is to search for local markets, try a couple of different brands, and stick with the merchants that seem to have the best.

Threads versus Powder

Saffron is available either as whole threads or as a powder composed of crushed threads. Many cooks prefer the powder because it is easier to measure, doesn't need to be steeped to release its color and flavoring, and doesn't clump together the way threads often do in sauces and batter. This is a personal choice. I like seeing the threads dotting the bread and floating on the surface of my broths. That's part of saffron's charm for me. But decide for yourself and use whatever you're most comfortable with.

Cost

The cost will be the same for both threads and powder, and although saffron is not as cheap as a bottle of peppercorns, it shouldn't be a king's ransom either. A small five-dollar-vial of good-quality saffron will be enough for several meals. A half-ounce jar of strong Macedonian Greek saffron that I bought earlier this year for twenty-five dollars and have used about a pinch from at least once a week since still has about two tablespoons left. On the other hand, a quarter-ounce pouch from Iran that cost fifteen dollars – and that I used just as often – is still half full simply because it is so strong that smaller pinches of it suffice.

Storing

Mass-produced saffron usually comes wrapped up like a Christmas present, complete with a ribbon or golden cord held in place by an official-looking seal. Smaller crops may come in little plastic pouches and should be poured into glass jars with secure lids as soon as possible to ensure that they stay fresh. Saffron stored away from heat and light, in as airtight a container as possible should retain its potency for several years.

Cooking with Saffron

If you have never cooked with saffron before, start out with something simple, like a Persian, Indian, or Italian rice dish. Iranian cooks use saffron in many dishes, but they add only a few threads because they are using it for its coloring and not its flavor. Indian cooks use a more generous pinch for a balance of flavor and color, much the same way Italian cooks use it in risotto recipes. If you can work your way up through these recipes, you'll soon discover the subtle differences a few threads make in coloring and flavor, and you will also learn your own personal preference for the spice. You can then feel safe turning to more complicated recipes.

Steeping

Remember that the threads are a dried substance; in order to release their flavor and coloring, they have to be rehydrated in either a hot, acidic, or alcoholic liquid (powdered saffron doesn't require this step). For any recipe that calls for saffron, your first step should be to steep the threads in the liquid so that by the time the recipe calls for their addition, the coloring and flavor will be at their height. Twenty minutes is the minimum time saffron should steep. As the threads soak, the liquid will slowly turn a bright yellow and orange; the heady scent will begin to permeate the kitchen. (If you're in a rush or have forgotten to steep the threads, try this: stir the saffron into whatever liquid the recipe calls for and microwave it for a minute or two [depending on quantity – one cup, for instance, should be microwaved for 1½ minutes].)

The Pinch

Many cooks stop dead in their tracks when a recipe calls for such an inexact quantity as a pinch of saffron. You're just going to have to figure the measurement out on your own, because the size of my pinch will never be the size of yours. Because saffron is such an organic, changeable substance, there is no other way to measure it. The best advice if you are not sure of either the saffron's strength or your taste is to use a very little – maybe ten to fifteen threads – and then go from there. If the color is not deep enough, or the flavor not as high as you wish, add a little more. You'll slowly learn what is your personal pinch size.

You just don't want to add too much. There is nothing as subtle and delicate as a small amount of saffron in a dish – intriguingly citric with a slight bitter edge. Too much, though, and it has a harsh medicinal flavor and smell you simply cannot get rid of. So be prudent and cautious: too much saffron is too much of a good thing.

Where to Use Saffron

Once you know and understand saffron, you'll find yourself using it in many different dishes. Nothing adds more zest to fish, custards, sauces, soups, and dough. If you add saffron toward the middle of the cooking, the flavor will be more subtle than if you add it toward the end. Baking seems to completely mellow the flavor out, making it almost sweet. Steeping in a cold liquid, such as vinegar or alcohol, gives the flavor a slight underlining note of hotness to it that makes for particularly interesting vinaigrettes and cocktails (particularly gin and vodka-based drinks).

Using Saffron as a Dye

Saffron is not a stable dye – it will wash out or fade very quickly – but, for a little while at least, it will produce a very intense shade of yellow, depending on how much saffron you use and for how long you steep the cloth in the bath. Prepare a dye bath by bringing water to a boil and throwing in a handful of saffron. Remove from heat. Let the saffron steep at least twenty minutes; then add whatever you wish to dye. When the color has developed to the shade you wish (actually, make it a little darker because some color will wash out in the rinse), take the fabric out, rinse it briefly, and hang it somewhere to dry that is away from direct sunlight. In the natural course of wearing, a saffron-dyed garment, as it is exposed to sunlight and washing, will gradually lose its color until it becomes a pale creamy shade.

Saffron will not only dye everything it touches but will leave its intense perfume behind. Paper soaked in saffron retains the scent for a very long time; on wood, saffron mingles with the natural oils buried in the wood to form a subtly different aroma.

Growing Your Own Saffron

I've found only two reliable sources for saffron corms:

1. *Saffron Walden Museum, Museum Street, Saffron Walden, Essex, CB10 1 JL; telephone: 01799 510333.*
2. *Brent and Becky's Bulbs, 7463 Heath Tral, Gloucester, VA 23061; (804) 693-3966.*

There are probably more places that sell saffron crocus corms, but the true *Crocus sativus* corms are hard to find, so be careful that you get the right bulbs.

The trick to growing saffron is in having a well-drained soil and an amply long growing season. Saffron will not tolerate heavy or damp soil, so be sure to mix in sand, chalk, or peat for drainage. Usually, the corms are planted in June and are harvested toward the middle of October. The corms are heavy feeders and will quickly drain nutrients from the soil, which was why old guide books advised lifting the corms every year or so and planting them in a new field, leaving old fields to renew themselves for as long as twenty years. We can now take advantage of modern fertilizers, but if you are serious about continuing a crop, you may have to let the fields rest after a couple of years; at the very least, you will certainly have to lift the corms up to divide them.

However, it's more important to choose a good site. Ideally, it should face south, receiving as much sunlight as possible throughout the day. Before you plant, hoe in nutrients – cow manure, compost, and leaf mold are all good. Plant the corms three inches deep and about three inches apart. Through the summer, keep the field free of weeds and water when the ground is dry. If autumn turns cold and frost threatens, cover the field any way you can. One light dusting of frost will quickly doom your crop.

Two Excellent Guides

For a more complete – and continually updated – guide, turn to Ellen Szita's Web site, www.saffroninfo.com. *The Essential Saffron Companion,* by John Humphries (Ten Speed Press, 1998), is another good source of general information.

Some Sources for Buying Saffron

Coupe and La Mancha Spanish saffron is available from Paseo de Castilla – La Mancha, 15-Bajo A 45720 Camunas (Toledo) Spain; telephone and fax: 925 47 02 48.

Kashmiri saffron is available from Penzeys LTD, PO Box 1448, Waukesha, WI 53187; (414) 574-0277. Another good source (though expensive) for Kashmiri saffron is Baby Brand Saffron, Uttam Singh, exporter, 6700, First Floor, Khari Baoli, Delhi, India 110 006. Baby Brand sells it over the Internet at www.babysaffron.com.

Organic Macedonian Greek saffron can be obtained on the Internet from Vanilla Saffron Imports at www.saffron.com or by writing 949 Valencia Street, San Francisco, CA 94110; (415) 648-8990.

Pennsylvania Dutch saffron is sold under the name Greider's saffron and is available at the Pennsylvania General Store in the Reading Terminal Market, Philadelphia, (800) 545-4891, or through their Web sites at www.pageneralstore.com.

Persian saffron is still illegal to import to the United States, but it can be obtained in New York City at Kalustyan's, 123 Lexington Avenue, New York, NY 10017 or through their Web site, www.kalustyans.com.

A Handful of Favorite Recipes

A few of these dishes I have mentioned throughout the book but didn't wish to break up the story by stopping to give directions. The first two are from Richard Stevens, a talented chef who, happily, lives up the street from me. The saffron consommé is from my previous book *A Soothing Broth,* but it is such a staple around the house both for dinner parties and to cure a cold that I felt there would be a hole in this book if I didn't list it here as well.

I have never claimed to be a good cook. This has little to do with modesty and much to do with tempering the expectations of anyone who will make the following recipes. That I often navigate the world from the kitchen, that there are few things sweeter to me than giving my family and friends something good to eat, seems sufficient reason, somehow, to share these recipes with others. I hope you find them as delicious as I do.

Richard's Saffron Lobster

Unlike most saffron recipes, this one requires that the saffron not be steeped in advance but instead be added directly to the oil. The saffron does not release very much flavor (which is why such a large amount is used) or color into the oil, but it does heat up a bit so that by the time the lobster hits it, the saffron seems ready to burst right into the shells. Whatever the precise chemical reaction that happens, the saffron comes to form a sort of gritty crust on the shells and across the skin that is simply awesome.

1 large live lobster (about 1½ to 2 pounds)
3 tablespoons olive oil
3 cloves of garlic, minced
a very large pinch (at least 100 threads, if not more) of saffron
½ cup fresh chicken stock (preferably homemade)
½ cup white wine
salt to taste
juice of 1 lemon

Pith the lobster by laying it on its stomach and quickly driving the sharp point of a thin-blade knife in the space directly behind the lobster's head. (The squeamish can quickly boil it until it's red, but the recipe turns out better if the lobster is pithed). Split the lobster in half down the middle. Discard the sack and vein, and reserve the liquid, roe, and tomalley. Set aside.

In a large, flat-bottom pan (a paella pan is perfect), heat the oil until hot over a medium-high burner. Add the garlic and sauté briefly; then add the saffron. Stir once to blend and add the lobster, meat side down. Cook for half a minute then turn over to the shell side. Cook for two minutes; then lower the heat. Add chicken stock (be careful – the hot oil may splatter when you add the stock), wine, and salt. When the liquid begins to simmer, cover the pan and let cook for about 10 minutes or until the lobster shell has turned red and the meat is firm and rosy. Add the lemon juice and stir to blend.

Serve on a bed of freshly made pasta with a little of the sauce poured over the noodles and the meat. Serves 4 for a main meal, 6 as a first course.

If you happen to have leftovers, the stock and meat make an incredible chowder in about 20 minutes. It is particularly heartwarming if you have served the saffron lobster the night before at a grand dinner party and are now contemplating a simple Sunday dinner that continues some of the elegance of the evening before. Prepare the following and I promise you you'll be in fine shape for the week ahead.

Finely chop a small onion and sauté it in about 2 tablespoons of sweet butter melted in a good size saucepan. Slowly add the leftover stock (if you have a lot of stock left over, then add about a cup to a cup and a half per serving). Stir to blend. Peel and dice two or three potatoes and add those to the stock. Simmer until the potatoes are tender. Chop up the left-over lobster meat and add to the stock. Simmer until the meat is heated through. At the last minute before serving, add some cream (heavy or light, it's a matter of taste and doesn't matter) – about half a cup to a quart of soup. Swirl to blend and gently heat; then serve immediately. Accompany the chowder with maybe a little salad, some crackers of toasted bread, and a glass of wine.

Portuguese Pork with Saffron

You can make this dish using a pork roast in much the same way as the sausage below; just cook the roast a little longer.

A pinch (about 40 threads) of saffron
½ cup white wine
1½ pounds Italian sausage, either hot or sweet, or a mixture of both
3 tablespoons olive oil
1 large garlic clove, minced
1 jalapeño pepper, sliced
juice of 1 lemon
½ cup chicken stock
3 dozen littleneck clams, scrubbed clean
handful of fresh cilantro leaves, chopped

Preheat oven to 400 degrees. Stir the saffron into the white wine and set aside to steep. Place the sausage in a shallow roasting pan and pour about a tablespoon of the oil over it. Place the pan in the oven and cook for about 30 to 40 minutes.

Remove the sausage and cut into serving pieces. Set aside. In the same pan, on top of the stove, add the remaining oil and over medium heat, sauté the garlic and pepper until the garlic turns golden and the pepper skin begins to blister.

Reduce the heat and add the saffron-infused wine (be careful – the oil may splatter). Stir, scraping up any meat or garlic pieces that might have stuck to the pan. Add the lemon juice, chicken stock, the reserved sausages, and the clams. Raise the heat to medium high, cover the pan, and let simmer until all the clams open.

Just before serving, stir in the cilantro. Serve over rice. Serves 6.

Saffron Consommé

Nothing takes the chill off of guests or makes a cold sufferer feel better – or well tended – faster than this consommé.

White stock:

5 pounds veal bones (including a knuckle), cracked
2 pounds chicken parts (backs, wings, or necks)
1 pound stewing veal, cut into 2-inch cubes
3 quarts water
1 large carrot, peeled, trimmed, and cut into 1-inch pieces
1 rib celery with tops, trimmed and cut into 1-inch pieces
1 medium leek, trimmed, cleaned, and cut into 1-inch pieces
1 onion, peeled and halved
6 sprigs parsley
2 teaspoons kosher salt
freshly ground pepper to taste

Put the bones, chicken, and veal into a large, 8-quart stockpot. Add enough water to cover by 2 inches. Bring to a boil, reduce heat, and simmer, uncovered, for 5 minutes.

Drain and rinse bones and meat under cold water to remove all the scum. Rinse and wipe the inside of the stockpot. Return meat and bones to the stockpot and add the 3 quarts of water. Bring to a boil over high heat, skimming often. Add the remaining ingredients. Reduce the heat, partially cover, and simmer gently for about 3 hours. Skim occasionally.

Strain the stock through a double layer of cheesecloth. The stock keeps, refrigerated and covered, for 3 or 4 days; or it can be frozen for up to 6 months. Skim the fat from the surface before using.

Consommé:

2 tablespoons grated onion
6 cups white stock, chilled and thoroughly skimmed of fat
2 large egg whites
2 eggshells, crushed
½ teaspoon saffron threads or ¼ teaspoon ground saffron
salt and freshly ground pepper to taste

Place the grated onion in a fine sieve over a small bowl and press down on it with the back of a spoon to extract the juices. Measure and set aside 1 teaspoon of the onion juice. Discard the rest.

In a 3-quart saucepan, bring the stock to a boil over high heat. Meanwhile, in a small bowl, whisk the egg whites until frothy. When the stock is boiling, stir in the egg whites and eggshells, reduce the heat, and simmer gently, without stirring, for about 20 minutes. Strain the stock into a slightly smaller stockpot through a large sieve lined with several thicknesses of rinsed cheesecloth. Bring to a simmer over moderate heat and stir in the reserved onion juice.

If you are using saffron threads, crush them between your fingers and place in a small dish. Add about ¼ cup of the hot stock, stir gently to dissolve the saffron, then pour the mixture into the simmering stock. If you are using ground saffron, whisk directly into the simmering stock.

Simmer for 3 to 5 minutes more to let the flavor develop. Add salt and pepper to taste. Makes 6 servings.

Michael's Seafood Cure

I've tried to come up with an approximation of the soup I was first served in that northern seaside town. I married the man I had fallen in love with and whom I turned Michael away for. When I served it to my husband one night when we were alone, he too was overwhelmed by its biting heat.

1 bottle of a good yeasty beer
a large pinch of saffron – about 60 threads
2 garlic cloves, crushed and minced
1 tablespoon olive oil
2 pounds of mixed shellfish, such as a small lobster or crayfish, shrimp, clams, mussels, scallops
coarse salt and pepper to taste

Pour the beer into a bowl and add the saffron. Let it steep a good half hour or more.

In a stockpot, over medium heat, sauté the garlic in the oil until it begins to turn brown. Remove the pot from the heat and layer in the shellfish in this manner: add clams and mussels on bottom, then the lobster, and finally the shrimp and scallops. Pour the beer over the shellfish (if the liquid doesn't cover at least three-fourths of the way up the shellfish, add a little more beer until it does). Place the pan back on the stove over medium-high heat and let cook until the clams and mussels open and the rest of the shellfish is either red or cooked through – about 20 minutes. Sprinkle coarse salt and pepper over the fish in the pot.

To serve: Send the kids over to your mom's house. Then bring the pot to the table and ladle a nice assortment of fish into deep bowls. Pour some of the broth over all. Have a plate of hearty crusty bread and a couple of cold beers on hand. Make a toast and dive in. Serves 2.

Saffron Tea

The following is really just a simple pick-me-up that I make if I'm having a subtly annoying day.

In a teacup of hot water, add a small pinch (15–20 threads) of saffron. Let it sit for about 10 minutes; then add a thin slice of lemon and a teaspoon of honey or sugar. Stir to mix. Reheat if desired (I pop it in the microwave for half a minute). Sip in a quiet place.

Saffron Custard

The egg custard comes from my mom; the saffron is just me.

2 cups light cream
pinch (40 threads) saffron
⅓ cup sugar
2 large eggs
1 large egg yolk
1½ teaspoons pure almond extract
boiling water

Preheat oven to 350 degrees. Place 4 custard cups or a medium-sized ovenproof glass dish in a shallow baking pan and set aside.

In a medium saucepan, heat the cream almost to the boiling point. Remove from heat and add the saffron and sugar; stir to dissolve the sugar. Let steep for 15 minutes. Meanwhile, in a mixing bowl, whisk the eggs with the yolk until smooth. With the beaters running, add the warm cream in a steady stream. Beat a half minute more; then add the almond extract.

Divide the custard among the cups or pour into the larger dish. Place the pan in the oven, then pour the boiling water around the cups or dish, making sure it reaches about two-thirds of the way up the sides. Bake until a knife inserted into the center of the custard comes out clean, about 30 minutes.

This is actually better served the next day – the flavor of the saffron seems to develop more fully after a rest. Serves 4.

Saffron Lemon Pound Cake

This is my winter cake. I usually make the first one sometime after the heat goes on for the first time in the house and always have it around for Christmas guests. The recipe makes one large cake or, divided in two, two loaf cakes.

For the glaze:
⅓ cup lemon juice
1 small pinch (about 15–20 threads) saffron
⅔ cup sugar
1 tablespoon grated lemon rind

For the cake:
Fine dry bread crumbs
1 cup milk
1 large pinch saffron (about 60 threads)
3 cups flour
2 teaspoons baking powder
¼ teaspoon salt
½ pound sweet butter, at room temperature
2 cups sugar
4 eggs
1 tablespoon grated lemon rind

Preheat oven to 325 degrees. Butter a 9-inch tube pan or two loaf pans. Coat the bottom and sides with the bread crumbs and set aside.

Stir all the ingredients for the glaze into a small bowl and set aside. Heat the milk in a small saucepan and when hot (but not boiling) remove from heat and stir in the saffron. Set aside for 20 minutes. Sift together the flour, baking powder, and salt in a medium bowl.

In a large bowl, cream the butter and sugar together; then beat the eggs in, one at a time. Alternate folding into the batter the dry ingredients with the milk. Stir the grated lemon rind into the batter. Pour the batter into the prepared pan. Bake for 1¼ hours or until a skewer inserted into the middle of the cake comes out clean.

Immediately remove cake from pan. Invert the cake onto a rack over a bowl and pour the glaze over the cake until all the glaze is absorbed.

INDEX